Ima Hogg

Ima Hogg

The Governor's Daughter

by
Virginia Bernhard

TexasMonthlyPress

Portions of Chapters 2 and 3 appeared in the *East Texas Historical Journal*, vol. 22, no. 1 (Spring 1984), and are reprinted here with the permission of the publisher.

Texas Monthly Press
P.O. Box 1569
Austin, Texas 78767

A   B   C   D   E   F   G   H

ISBN 0-932012-68-X

Library of Congress Cataloging in Publication Data

Bernhard, Virginia, 1937–
    Ima Hogg: the governor's daughter.

    1. Hogg, Ima.   2. Art patrons — Texas — Biography.
3. Texas — Governors — Children — Biography.   I. Title.
N5220.H62B4 1984   976.4'06'0924 [B]   83-24266

Contents

Preface

Ima Hogg, who died at ninety-three while on a trip to London in 1975, was something of a legend in her own time. She was one of the country's leading collectors of Early American antiques, and Bayou Bend, the American Decorative Arts Wing of the Museum of Fine Arts, Houston, is one of the nation's finest repositories of American decorative arts. But Ima Hogg's earliest ambition was to be a concert pianist, not a collector, and Bayou Bend was built as a home for her and her brothers, not as a museum. Thereby hangs a tale — one that is a significant chapter in the cultural life of the Southwest, as well as the history of the Hogg family.

James Stephen Hogg, who worked his way from the red dirt farmland of East Texas to the Governor's Mansion in Austin and named his only daughter Ima for reasons that perhaps only he could explain, was one of the most colorful and controversial public figures in Texas history. He left his children — Will, Ima, Mike, and Tom — a fortune in oil under the Gulf Coast plain near West Columbia, and they used the larger part of it for the enrichment of the educational and cultural life of their state. But except for a political biography of Governor Hogg and some short sketches of Ima and Will, the history of the Hogg family has been mostly hearsay. Many people in Texas still believe, for example, that Governor Hogg had daughters named Ima and Ura, and sons named Moore and Harry.

This book is an effort to set at least part of the record straight, and to set down some of the things that Ima Hogg, for all her passion for history and her devotion to her family, never had time to put on paper — and some things, perhaps, that she never would have. Ima Hogg once said that she never wanted her biography written, and her personal papers in the Eugene C. Barker Texas History Center at the University of Texas at Austin are still not open for general use. But the story of the Hoggs — Governor Hogg, the three-hundred-pound giant of Texas politics in the 1890s; his blustery, bighearted son Will; his younger sons, Mike, earnest and determined to carry on the family traditions, and Tom, charming and irresponsible; and his only daughter, Ima, who became a "collector of people" as well as a nationally prominent collector of antiques, a patron of the arts, and a founder of the Houston Symphony—can be told at least in part. More than anything else, the history of the Hogg family is the story of Ima Hogg, the little girl born in 1882 in Mineola, Texas, who grew up to be—to use the old-fashioned expression—a great lady.

Before her death Ima Hogg had begun work on a memoir of her childhood and her life as Governor Jim Hogg's daughter. This book makes use of some of those recollections, as well as the letters, diaries, and scrapbooks of clippings in the Hogg papers in Austin and in the archives at Bayou Bend. Most of the people who knew Ima Hogg's father and brothers are gone now, but many of those who knew "Miss Ima" were kind enough to share their recollections of her with me. Some of the people who worked closely with Ima Hogg over the years—John Staub, the architect of Bayou Bend; Charles Montgomery of Winterthur; Charles Cornelius, the first curator of the American Wing of the Metropolitan Museum of Art; Henry Francis du Pont, the creator of Winterthur—are themselves no longer living, and their contributions to Ima Hogg's work have been reconstructed from their correspondence and from the recollections of others. Felide Robertson, longtime friend of Ima Hogg, former Bayou Bend docent chairman, and the collection's librarian, contributed countless anecdotes, verified bits of elusive information, and provided much of the momentum for this work. Geraldine Styles, archivist at Bayou Bend, was most generous with her time and her energy. David Warren, the first curator of Bayou Bend, offered encouragement in the early stages of the project. Three people who deserve special mention are Jane Zivley, Ima Hogg's secretary for twenty-five years; Yvonne Coates Kleinsorge, her nurse-companion during her last years; and William Lee Pryor, a close friend. Others whose recollections proved invaluable are Tom M. Johnson, Sandy Thompson, Nettie Jones, Faith Bybee, Mary Fuller, Barry Greenlaw, Harold Sack, Bernard Levy, Dean Failey, Ralph Carpenter, and Jonathan Fairbanks. A word of thanks is also due to Barbara Day, Prim Specht, Betty Ring, Douglas McDugald, Elizabeth Moore, W. B. Ferguson, Chester Kielman, Elva Kalb Dumas, Ann Holmes, and Carl Cunningham, to Meg Romano and A. J. Marsh for preparation of the final manuscript, to Chris Kindschi, my editor, and to the staffs of the Houston Metropolitan Research Center, the Barker Texas History Center of the University of Texas at Austin, Fondren Library at Rice University, and Doherty Library at the University of St. Thomas.

University of St. Thomas
January 1983

1

Miss Ima

At three minutes past five o'clock on the afternoon of August 14, 1975, the London rush hour traffic had begun to clog the wide lanes of Brompton Road, and a chilly rain was falling. In the crowds of pedestrians, umbrellas began to sprout like so many black mushrooms. The two women who had just finished shopping at Harrods had no umbrella, and they waved in vain at several taxis before one with its "For Hire" flag up pulled over to the curb. As the women hurried to get inside, the vehicle suddenly rolled forward, and the unexpected movement threw one of them off balance. A younger and nimbler person might have avoided injury, but the one climbing into the cab that rainy afternoon was Miss Ima Hogg, age ninety-three. The trim London Fog trench coat and the soft felt hat atop carefully coiffed hair belied her years, but her movements were, as she herself confessed, no longer agile.

Although Ima Hogg's zest for travel was as keen as it had been at sixteen when she and her father, Texas governor James Stephen Hogg, had sailed to Hawaii to watch the United States flag raised over the islands in 1898, she had made a few concessions to age. One was the collapsible wheelchair beside her on the pavement. Of late she had taken to using it to conserve her strength on long excursions, and she found it indispensable for travel. Waiting in a ticket line in front of Albert Hall, she napped in it; wheeling around the National Gallery, she rolled cheerily past throngs of footsore tourists; shopping in it at Harrods or at Fortnum & Mason, gesturing regally with her cane, she seldom waited long for service. This afernoon she and her traveling companion, Yvonne Coates, had gone to Harrods to look for some tortoiseshell combs for her hair, but they had not found exactly what they wanted.

Now Ima Hogg had fallen under the open door of the taxi and could not get up. As the frantic cab driver summoned an ambulance and

1

Ima Hogg

Mrs. Coates tried to make her as comfortable as she could be, lying on the pavement in the rain, she reclined on the curb, her hat still at its original jaunty angle and her self-possession undamaged. "Don't worry," she said, "I can't move just now, but it's going to be all right." Passersby had begun to surround them. An elderly man selling flowers from a pushcart around the corner brought the tarpaulin cover from his cart to tuck around her. A well-dressed gentleman in a dark suit and a bowler hat stopped and held his large black umbrella over her. Ima Hogg thanked them graciously in her soft Southern accent, as though they were offering her a parasol and a chair at a garden party.

Five days later, on Tuesday, August 19, in London's Westminster Hospital, Ima Hogg died. Although she had survived surgery on her fractured hip, in the end her heart failed. To a friend who had recently cautioned her about the hazards of transatlantic travel for a nonagenarian, she had said lightly, "When you're ninety-three, it doesn't matter where you die." In Houston, where Ima Hogg had lived for more than six decades, the *Houston Post* announced her death with a front-page banner headline. The same afternoon the *Houston Chronicle* carried the story of her death under page-one headlines and a four-column picture of her in evening clothes arriving at a Houston Symphony opening. Across the rest of the nation, 291 other papers noted the passing of Ima Hogg. It was certainly not the first time she had been in the news. The *New York Times*' Charlotte Curtis had once said of her, "She is to Houston what Alice Roosevelt Longworth is to Washington and Mrs. Lytle Hull to New York." *Time* magazine had called her "Empress of the Symphony" and "one of the grandest of all musical *grandes dames* in the U.S."

In Houston a grieving staff at Bayou Bend, the American Decorative Arts Wing of the Museum of Fine Arts, made mournful preparations for a funeral service. Bayou Bend, a pink stucco mansion on the banks of Buffalo Bayou, had been Ima Hogg's home for nearly forty years. She had not intended for the house to become a museum, but in the late 1950s she had had to make a decision: "I had been collecting American furniture. I collected, and collected, and collected, until I had so much of it I didn't know what to do with it. I decided to give it as a museum. I said I would; they said they would take it—if *I* endowed it. I wasn't smart. I said, 'All right, if you'll match me.' But they didn't." So she gave it anyway.

Ima Hogg spent half a century putting together the Bayou Bend Collection, creating a museum that is said by some to be second only to Henry Francis du Pont's Winterthur. ("Oh, my, what I could do if I had his money!" she once said.) Along the way, she also managed to

2

found the Houston Symphony Society (1913), establish the Houston Child Guidance Clinic (1929), organize the Hogg Foundation for Mental Health (1940), and win election to the Houston Board of Education (1943), where she initiated the Houston Symphony's student concerts and worked to establish art programs in the city's then-segregated black high schools. In her seventies and eighties she restored and gave to the State of Texas several antebellum buildings, including a plantation house at West Columbia and a stagecoach inn near Round Top, personally directing the restoration of all of them down to the last hand-hewn nail. Always self-effacing, sometimes shy, she would never admit that she had been the driving force in the cultural life of a city and a state for the greater part of the twentieth century.

"As the physical needs of the state are being fulfilled," Ima Hogg once said, "(I know you can't ask a starving child to paint a pretty picture) we need to think more about the things that make life worth living, the nourishing of the spirit." Her own contributions to that nourishment were rich and varied. The paintings, the lithographs and sketches, the Indian artifacts and dolls she collected over the years and gave to the Museum of Fine Arts; the treasures of American decorative art and the gardens at Bayou Bend; the concerts by the Houston Symphony; the University of Texas center for Texas history and ethnic studies at the old German community of Winedale in the Hill Country are only part of Ima Hogg's efforts "to make life worth living."

She was concerned not only with the nourishing of the spirit but with the health of the mind as well. Looking back on her many interests, she said in 1974 that the one that had given her the most pleasure was her part in establishing the Houston Child Guidance Clinic. The clinic was designed to provide counseling and therapy for children with emotional problems, and it now offers individual and group treatment for children ages one to eighteen and their families. In addition, the Ima Hogg Therapeutic School now provides a one-to-one teacher-pupil ratio for students who are unable to learn in a conventional classroom setting.

Ima Hogg always liked a project with tangible, immediate results, whether it happened to be the restoration of an old house or the rehabilitation of a disturbed child. In 1940 she established the Hogg Foundation for Mental Health at the University of Texas at Austin. It was not just for research, she insisted, but for helping people directly. One of the foundation's early projects was to send lecturers on mental health to the small towns and rural areas of Texas. Ima Hogg envisioned these speakers as a "new type of circuit rider" who would

3

bring the latest scientific knowledge to people who might otherwise never hear about it. Mental health was a subject that had fascinated Ima Hogg since the turn of the century, when, as a coed at the University of Texas, she had studied psychology with Dr. A. Caswell Ellis. While her father, James Stephen Hogg, was governor of Texas from 1891 to 1895, she had occasionally visited state institutions for the mentally ill, and she had never forgotten what she saw. Years afterward, when time and resources permitted, she resolved to do what she could to advance the cause of mental health in Texas.

From 1940 until her death in 1975, Ima Hogg maintained an active interest in the work of the Hogg Foundation, and that organization, like the Houston Symphony Orchestra and Bayou Bend, owes much to her remarkable dedication and energy. "She was never idle — never," her nurse-companion, Yvonne Coates, recalled several years after her death. Even in her nineties she kept Jane Zivley, her personal secretary for twenty-five years, busy from eight to five Monday through Friday and from one to two on Saturdays. In spare moments she kept a watchful eye on the helter-skelter growth of Houston, opposing the building of a stadium here, campaigning for the preservation of hundred-year-old oak trees there, and refusing to allow drilling for oil in Memorial Park, a gift from the Hogg family to the City of Houston. She wrote letters to congressmen and city councilmen and newspaper editors on subjects ranging from the need for a new concert hall to a suggestion for a day of prayer for world peace. On December 1, 1950, she sent a telegram to senators Lyndon Johnson and Tom Connally: "Please plead against use of atomic bomb. We must consider future. Protest such terrible example would act as boomerang bringing untold destruction to ourselves and entire world."

In cultural affairs Ima Hogg was devoted to the Houston Symphony Orchestra, serving twelve terms as Symphony Society president and pronouncing shrewdly and knowledgeably on affairs both artistic and financial. Nothing was too small or too large for her concern, from the supply of Coca-Cola in the Music Hall lobby to the last-minute replacement of a disaffected conductor with Sir Thomas Beecham: "He was very gracious. We feel elated," she said modestly. It was Ima Hogg in later years who was mainly responsible for luring Leopold Stokowski and Sir John Barbirolli to the Houston podium. "I was not," she once remarked, "going to have a one-horse orchestra." When Houston's newspaper critics were less than complimentary to the symphony on occasion, she berated them for impeding its progress. Ann Holmes, fine arts editor of the *Houston Chronicle*, recalled an early encounter with the symphony's staunchest defender: "She invited me

4

to her house, sat me in a chair, turned a bright lamp in my face, and *grilled* me." When *Houston Post* critic Carl Cunningham wrote an unfavorable review just before a symphony maintenance fund drive, Miss Ima gave him a ceremonial whack with her cane, saying, "How *dare* you do that to us!"

Although Ima Hogg herself refrained from passing artistic judgment on the symphony in public, in private she was its most exacting critic. In fact, as she grew older, symphonygoers within hearing distance of her box might hear an irascible whisper that the second movement of the *Eroica* was too slow or that the strings in the Brahms Fourth were a bit ragged. But she never interfered in the artistic side, and she never questioned the programming. If anything, her preferences ran to the modern, the avant garde. "There was nothing old-fashioned about Miss Ima," Tom M. Johnson, the Houston Symphony's general manager from 1948 to 1973, once said. "In the early 1950s, when the Dave Brubeck jazz quartet first came here for a concert, she went. The next time I saw her she said, 'And where were *you* at the Brubeck concert?' " In the 1960s Ima Hogg startled some of her friends by becoming an avid Beatles fan. In the 1970s, conductor Lawrence Foster, criticized for programming too much atonal modern music, remarked wryly that Miss Ima, then in her eighties, was the only one who appreciated it.

In 1972, in her ninetieth year, the Houston Symphony paid tribute to Ima Hogg with a special birthday concert. There was champagne and cake; Arthur Rubinstein played the piano; and three thousand people sang "Happy Birthday." Miss Ima, resplendent in a brocade gown of pale apricot and silver and wearing antique aquamarine jewelry, spoke briefly. She thanked the audience for their continuing support of the orchestra and for the party, adding, "I feel, however, it is I who should have given the party in honor of you." Earlier in the day her household staff had fussed over her because she had a bad cold and they feared she would not be able to make her appearance. "It will be all right," she said. "I don't have to *sing*."

Afterward there was a party with Rubinstein, who was then nearly ninety himself, as Ima Hogg's dinner partner. They smiled, they chatted, they posed for dozens of photographs. Privately, however, neither was much impressed by the other. Before the gala evening began, the irrepressible Rubinstein had confided to an associate: "I had to sit next to Ima Hogg last year at an awards ceremony at Southwestern University. She's a tiresome old woman, isn't she?" Said Ima Hogg about Arthur Rubinstein, some while after the dinner party, "What a pompous old man!" In 1975, when Vladimir Horowitz played

5

Ima Hogg

an Easter Sunday concert in Houston, Miss Ima appeared backstage afterward with a small package. It was, she said, "a little present for Mr. Horowitz. Such a nice man. Not at all like that Mr. Rubinstein."

There was one thing, however, that Arthur Rubinstein and Ima Hogg had in common: a fine disregard for advancing old age. John F. Staub, the architect who designed Bayou Bend in the late 1920s and who was Ima Hogg's close friend for nearly fifty years afterward, said that she "just flowered" in later life: "She was younger at her death, Ima was, than when I first knew her." When Staub and Miss Ima first met, she was somewhat shy and retiring. In later years, however, the mistress of Bayou Bend became at once more imperious and more adventuresome. "When you're as old as I am," she announced at age ninety-two, "you can do anything you want to!" In her eighties, she climbed up into an old church balcony in Round Top to play the organ; in her nineties, outfitted in rose-colored culottes, she pedaled a tricycle down the hall of her apartment building to cheer up a convalescing friend. Attending a museum board meeting, she brought along her Chihuahua dog, Ludie (for Ludwig von Beethoven), and sat with him on her lap. Watching the circus, she demanded to meet the lion tamer. Traveling in Germany in her nineties, she refused to hire a car and opted instead to climb on and off buses with the rest of the tourists. Waiting at Kennedy International Airport, she accosted a young man with shoulder-length hair: "Young man, would you mind talking to me?" she began. "I find your hair most attractive. . . . " As it happened, the young man was a musician from Boston, and the two had an agreeable chat, each charmed by the other.

As she grew older Ima Hogg continued to follow an itinerary that would have taxed a person half her years, making annual rounds of Europe's museums and concert halls (a gala ninetieth-birthday celebration at Round Top in the summer of 1972 had to be held early because she would be sailing on the *Queen Elizabeth 2* on July 10, her actual birthday); flying to New York to visit the Steinway piano factory to select the concert grand she presented to the Houston Symphony; hunting for Early American antiques in New England (on her way to London in 1975 she had detoured to Boston to see the Paul Revere exhibit at the Museum of Fine Arts and to lunch with her longtime friend, curator Jonathan Fairbanks); and driving around Texas to do research on her memoirs. An account of her early years as the only daughter of Governor James Stephen Hogg — the beginning of what might have been her autobiography — lies unfinished among her personal papers. It was to have been her next project when she returned from Europe. A friend had cautioned Yvonne Coates when Ima Hogg

6

engaged her as a companion: "Ima," she said, "will wear you out." From 1913 until her death, she kept a daybook with an hourly schedule of appointments and activities. It was seldom blank.

Ima Hogg delighted in the practical (at ninety, she bought a green wool pantsuit with a matching beret for travel) and in the efficient (when individual packets of instant soup appeared on the market she kept a constant supply, calling it "paper soup"). When wigs became fashionable she wore one with great amusement over her own light blonde hair. Elegantly and stylishly dressed (she was fond of hats and soft pale colors that set off her fair complexion and vivid blue eyes) and, despite her diminutive five-foot-two-inch height, imposing of manner ("Audiences at concerts parted before her like the Red Sea," said a friend), Ima Hogg was the nearest thing Texas had to royalty. An invitation to her home, as Tom Johnson once observed, was "like an invitation to Buckingham Palace."

Since 1966, with Ima Hogg's gift of her home to the Museum of Fine Arts, that invitation has been open to all. Bayou Bend, with its twenty-two elegant rooms and fourteen acres of elaborate gardens, is a pale pink stucco mansion of vaguely Georgian style built on the edge of River Oaks, Houston's most prestigious residential neighborhood. The land borders Buffalo Bayou, a meandering brown stream that winds its way three miles eastward to a site in downtown Houston known as Allen's Landing. Here in 1836 the Allen brothers, two land speculators from New York, arrived and decided it was a good place to build a city. In that city, a bumptious young oil-rich metropolis by the 1920s, the Hogg family (themselves newly wealthy from oil) built Bayou Bend in 1927. The house was to be a home for Ima, then forty-five, and her bachelor brothers, Will, eight years her senior, and Mike, three years younger than she. Tom, the youngest of the Hogg children, was married and living in San Antonio.

The two elder Hogg brothers were occupied with oil and real estate interests, and so it was Ima who saw to the design of Bayou Bend. Working closely with Staub, who had just arrived from New York, she planned a house to set off the American antiques she had already begun to collect. Bayou Bend was never intended as anything but a private house, but as Ima Hogg's interest in American antiques grew and as she acquired more and more pieces it became all too obvious that there was no museum space in Houston large enough to house the contents of Bayou Bend. And so in 1956 she decided to give to the public not only her collection but the very house she lived in.

There was a time when the giving of one's house to posterity as a museum was almost a habit among the makers of the great American fortunes, and visitors now file regularly through imposing structures to gaze at rooms that once belonged to steel tycoons, railroad barons, and oil magnates. Bayou Bend, however, is not one of these. Conceived, designed, and arranged by its owner, it retains a personal quality that sets it apart from Andrew Carnegie's home (now New York's Cooper-Hewitt Museum of Decorative Arts and Design) and the Henry Huntington house (now the Huntington Library and Art Gallery at San Marino, California) and many other house-museums across the country. The one that Bayou Bend most resembles is a museum that surpasses it in size, but not in style: Henry Francis du Pont's family home at Winterthur, near Wilmington, Delaware. Winterthur, with almost two hundred period rooms dating from 1640 to 1840, houses the largest and finest collection of American antiques in the world. But Bayou Bend, as one antiques dealer remarked, is "a distillation of Winterthur." Smaller and more gracious than the rambling nine-story structure set into a hillside at Winterthur, Bayou Bend is less tiring (two-hour tours as opposed to four-hour ones) and perhaps easier for the average museum visitor to absorb. There are many rare pieces at Bayou Bend; an elaborately carved mahogany corner chair made in New York between 1760 and 1780 may be the only one left of its kind. Some are masterpieces (among them, a magnificent block-front, shell-carved mahogany kneehole dressing table from Newport, Rhode Island, made between 1760 and 1785) that rival those at Winterthur and in the Metropolitan Museum of Art; the Museum of Fine Arts, Boston; and the Philadelphia Museum of Art.

Bayou Bend is unusual among American museums of its kind in that it does not charge admission. Ima Hogg wanted it that way. She did not want the public to have to pay to see Bayou Bend, just as she did not want the "little man in the balcony" to have to pay too high a price for his Houston Symphony tickets. While groups of 25 to 150 pay from $50 to $100 for special tours, admission is free to visitors on the regular tours. All visitors to Bayou Bend must make reservations in advance, however, and most leave something in the discreetly placed glass cube labeled "Contributions" in the cottage where they meet the museum docents who serve as tour guides. Nearly 55,000 visitors a year walk through the house and gardens of Bayou Bend. At Christmas the rooms are resplendent and fragrant with candles and decorations of pine needles and magnolia leaves, and choirs of schoolchildren sing carols. On two weekends every March Bayou Bend is the highlight of the River Oaks Garden Club's annual Azalea Trail, as the gardens there show off their hundreds of azaleas in every hue from deepest fuchsia to palest white. But now, on Saturday afternoons during the Azalea Trail tours, the strains of the Metropolitan Opera matinee no longer float down from the radio in the Queen Anne Sitting Room on the second floor as they did when Miss Ima lived there.

To walk through the rooms of Bayou Bend today is to experience, as fully as it is possible to do so, the lifestyles of the past, and to share the aesthetics of generations of earlier Americans. Admittedly, the original owners of most of Bayou Bend's treasures were upper-class Americans. The elegance of carved mahogany, the delicate tracery of porcelain, the glow of burnished brass, bespeak a certain affluence, then as now. These are rooms where Cotton Mather, Thomas Jefferson, or Andrew Jackson would have felt at home. It has been said that to arrive at even a general impression of a historical era, one must study not only what was written but also what was sat upon, eaten from, ridden on, and lived in and with. There are few places in America where the years from the colonial period to the antebellum era come alive as they do at Bayou Bend.

Most of these places, however, are in the East. Perhaps that is because Chippendale highboys and porcelain tea sets did not travel well in covered wagons. Except for Ima Hogg, the major collectors of American antiques for many years were also in the East. She served as a magnet, drawing some of the finest pieces to Bayou Bend — and keeping them there. She was always adamant in her refusals to lend something from the Bayou Bend Collection to exhibits in New York or New England. "They've got plenty of these things up there," she would say. She kept her "things" for Texas.

Although there is a Texas Room at Bayou Bend, Ima Hogg made a conscious effort to avoid provincialism. At the dedication of Bayou Bend in 1966 she said, "Texas, an empire in itself, geographically and historically sometimes seems to be regarded as remote or alien to the rest of the nation. I hope in a modest way Bayou Bend may serve as a bridge to bring us closer to the heart of an American heritage which unites us." Jonathan Fairbanks, curator of the American collection of the Museum of Fine Arts, Boston, once remarked that Ima Hogg's taste and aesthetic judgment had made her museum an art collection and not just "a gathering of historical relics." The late Charles Montgomery, Senior Research Fellow at Winterthur, called Bayou Bend "the largest, finest collection this side of Winterthur." Ima Hogg, showered with praise at the dedication ceremonies, observed wryly that she could hardly recognize herself. When her turn came to speak she modestly insisted, "I would rather not call Bayou Bend a museum. I think that is too pretentious. But I do hope the collection is of museum quality."

Ima Hogg

From the first piece in the collection, an eighteenth-century American chair bought in 1920, Miss Ima spent over fifty years satisfying her "unaccountable compulsion," as she called it, to collect pieces that were of museum quality. "It is said that collecting is a disease," she once said. "I think I had it from childhood." A close friend, Nettie Jones, recalled how Ima Hogg, when an ear condition kept her from traveling by air, took trains to New York and New England to find what she wanted. "Once," said Mrs. Jones, "I put her on the train to Boston. She went all the way to Boston and back — just for one glass bottle." The years passed, but Ima Hogg's enthusiasm for collecting never waned. David Warren, the first curator of Bayou Bend, later associate director of the Museum of Fine Arts, Houston, said, "She had a God-given eye for excellence — not just for furniture, but for everything. If you put her on a desert island with nothing but a few pebbles, in a little while she would have collected a handful of the best ones — the ones most remarkable for their essential qualities of pebbleness."

In the early 1900s, when many Americans were still absorbing the artistic shocks of the Ashcan School and the 1911 Armory Show that rocked New York with paintings like Marcel Duchamp's *Nude Descending a Staircase*, Ima Hogg was buying Picassos and Chagalls. "They are so old hat now," she said modestly in the 1960s, "that even people who do not like modern art like them." In 1939 she gave eighty-four originals to the Museum of Fine Arts, Houston, including a Sargent watercolor, two Millet etchings, four lithographs and two etchings by Picasso (one of the latter is a study for a later work, *The Absinthe Drinker*), a color lithograph by Cézanne entitled *The Bathers*, etchings by Matisse, Manet, and Maillol, a pen-and-ink sketch by Modigliani, three Dürer woodcuts, watercolors by Klee, and a lithograph by Diego Rivera called *The Fruits of Labor*. In 1944 Ima Hogg gave her collection of American Indian art to the museum: 168 pieces of pottery, 95 pieces of jewelry, 81 paintings, and 123 Kachina dolls made by the Zuñi and Hopi tribes.

In the 1940s and 1950s she concentrated on collecting American antiques, and although Ima Hogg lived in Texas, she managed to hold her own in the competition of major collectors then active in the East: Electra Webb, the Henry Flynts, Katharine Prentis Murphy, Henry Ford, and Henry Francis du Pont — all of whom were creating their own museums, and who had the advantage of access to the East, where most of the antiques were. Ima Hogg made trips to New York dealers' showrooms once or twice a year and kept up a steady correspondence with the major dealers. Harold Sack, of Israel Sack, Inc., recalled her as "very sharp. A good businesswoman — and a hard trader. When rare pieces came into this showroom," said Sack, "she could *smell* them!" Once when Sack and his brother had been to an auction in a small Connecticut town and had brought back an extremely rare eighteenth-century New York–made corner chair with a carved back, word of the find traveled quickly around the collectors' grapevine. Henry du Pont contacted the Sacks about the chair, but while he was making up his mind, said Sack, "In walked Miss Ima. 'Where is it?' she said. 'Where is *what*, Miss Ima?' I said. 'The chair,' she said, and made a deal on the spot."

She did not buy by instinct, however. She studied; she amassed a library of nearly a thousand volumes on every aspect of antiques and decorative arts; and when the Williamsburg Antiques Forums began in the 1950s, she was an avid participant. One of the things Ima Hogg loved best was to drive through New England on her own, looking for pieces. She and her secretary, Jane Zivley, would rent a car and set out. "When I asked if I should not see the road map," said Mrs. Zivley, "she would always say no, she knew where we were going. We drove all over New England — lost most of the time." That, however, did not bother Miss Ima, who liked to lean out her side of the car from time to time and ask directions of passersby.

Miss Ima inspired a fierce loyalty among those who knew her. After her death, her secretary guarded her memory and her private papers with meticulous care; Yvonne Coates Kleinsorge, her nurse and companion for the last three years of her life, was equally cautious. "Well," she would say, "I'm not sure she would want me to talk about *that*." More than one close friend interviewed for this book could not speak of her without coming near to tears. Her household staff — Lucious Broadnax, her butler-chauffeur, and Gertrude Vaughn, her personal maid — had been with her for decades, Broadnax since the 1930s and Vaughn since the 1920s. Dean Failey, a former curatorial assistant at Bayou Bend, called Ima Hogg a collector of people.

Her powers of persuasion were legendary. Yvonne Coates Kleinsorge recalled that when she came to Houston in the early 1970s to visit her sister, she had no intention of applying for a position as a companion to a ninety-year-old woman. Her sister, however, persuaded her to go for an interview with Ima Hogg, "just to see what she is like." "Well, I did," said Mrs. Kleinsorge. "She was lying on a couch, and she looked at me with those blue eyes — she had the prettiest, bluest eyes I'd ever seen, and skin just like a baby's — and she said, 'I want you.' I hadn't planned on going to work for her, but she talked me into it just like that. We became very close. I'm not sure

11

who was a companion to whom. I took care of her when she needed things, but in many ways, *I* leaned on *her*."

When Ima Hogg wanted something, or when she was on the trail of something she wanted for her collections, she could sugarcoat her single-mindedness with layers of charm, so that people dealing with her found themselves agreeing to things they never intended. Once when she was traveling through North Carolina in the summer of 1966, she discovered a collection of exquisite early nineteenth-century mourning embroideries in a little shop in Chapel Hill. Mourning embroideries, fashionable wall hangings in the sentimental nineteenth century, were intricately stitched needlework memorials to the death of a loved one. Some embroideries might have a replica of the tombstone and its inscription; others showed urns and weeping figures under a willow tree. Those in the Chapel Hill shop were especially fine, done in silk thread and watercolors on silk fabric. Enchanted by them, Miss Ima was distressed to learn that they were not for sale. The owner of the shop was herself a collector, and one of the embroideries had been an anniversary present from her husband, she said, so she could never part with it. Fifteen minutes with Ima Hogg and she changed her mind. All three of the mourning embroideries, including the anniversary gift, now hang in the west upstairs hall at Bayou Bend.

Antique dealers as well as collectors often found themselves subject to Ima Hogg's imperatives. When New York dealer Bernard Levy and his wife stopped in Houston on their way to Florida on vacation to deliver a rare Empire table she had bought, she entertained them for several days at Bayou Bend. On the morning that the Levys were ready to set out for Florida, she announced that she wanted them "to drive over and look at something I've found" before they left. As Levy recalled, "She then insisted that we see Round Top, telling us that it would be on our way to Florida. So . . . we went out to Round Top [a distance of some eighty miles], which I then discovered was in the wrong direction. We had lunch in a little local place, where Miss Hogg brought dessert and salad, and everyone had a wonderful time. When I realized the extra distance, my wife and I had a good laugh to see how persuasive she actually was, but in any case, it really was a dictate from above."

On the evening of Ima Hogg's ninetieth birthday party at Round Top, a gala striped-tent supper party for three hundred guests, she persuaded Harold Sack, who had come down from New York to surprise her, to go and look at another of her finds. It had been a long and tiring evening for Sack, who had flown from New York and driven from Houston to Round Top that afternoon. Ima Hogg, attired in a high-necked dress of yards of pink chiffon, had circulated among her guests for several hours. "I hope you all live as long as I do and enjoy life as much as I have," she said. About nine o'clock in the evening, as the crowd thinned, she began to look for Harold Sack. "I thought maybe she would be too tired, or would forget about it," said Sack, "and I hoped she would. I had the drive back to Houston still to make that night. But she never forgot anything." With Ima and her portable wheelchair in a station wagon, Sack and a small entourage set out for the antebellum house she was then restoring and furnishing. "The house had high front steps," Sack remembered, "and there were no lights, and we had to carry Miss Ima and her wheelchair up and into the house." By candlelight, the party viewed the object of their visit: a ponderous carved four-poster bed of black walnut. "It had wings and cherubs and everything else all over it," said Sack. "So I said, 'Miss Ima, I have never seen anything like that in my life.' 'No,' said Miss Hogg with great satisfaction, 'and you never will again, either.' "

People generally did as Ima Hogg asked them. Jonathan Fairbanks recalled the time when he was a new graduate of the Program in Early American Culture at Winterthur. Ima Hogg invited him to come and train the first group of museum docents at Bayou Bend in 1961. "Of course, at first I was not that familiar with the collection," said Fairbanks, "but when I got there, she pinned a microphone on me and announced that everything I said would be taped and printed as a booklet for future docent classes." Ima Hogg had already handpicked the first volunteer class of twenty-two women, and with them she attended the thrice-weekly sessions of room studies that Fairbanks gave. Before each session, she and Fairbanks would meet the docent class in the central hallway of Bayou Bend, and then she would announce what room they were to study that day. Sometimes the choice was a surprise, even to Fairbanks. There were a few times when he found out only moments beforehand what the subject of his two-hour lecture was to be. Ima Hogg, a challenging gleam in her eye, would accompany the group to the designated room, where she listened approvingly to the lecture and occasionally corrected the lecturer.

In January 1965 Miss Ima invited David Warren, another Winterthur graduate, to come to Houston for a stay at Bayou Bend and an interview for the job of curator. Warren had impressive credentials — an undergraduate degree from Princeton and an M.A. from the Winterthur Early American Culture program — but he was only twenty-eight years old, and he had doubts at first about passing Ima

Hogg's inspection. He arrived and was shown to his room to freshen up, and then was instructed to come to the Queen Anne Sitting Room where Miss Hogg would see him. As he remembered his first encounter with the mistress of Bayou Bend, "She was small and dainty and feminine — and smart and sharp and knowledgeable — all rolled into one." Later she invited Warren into what is now the Maple Bedroom and summoned Lucious Broadnax, her butler, to "bring in a chair for Mr. Warren." The chair was not to sit on but to examine. It was a simple chair with turned legs and a rush seat, and he described its fine points and analyzed it as eloquently and knowledgeably as he could, as he said, "shaking in my boots all the while." When he had exhausted the chair's origins and attributes, Ima Hogg said abruptly, "Do you smoke?"

"No," said the somewhat bewildered Warren.

"Do you drink?"

"Yes."

"Why?" she asked.

Warren answered rather lamely, "I like it, I suppose."

"Very well," said Ima Hogg, "thank you."

That ended the first interview. A short time afterward she offered David Warren the position as curator of Bayou Bend. Said Warren: "There wasn't a time I didn't learn something from her, not just about my field, but about life in general. Even if I had done research on a subject, I found out she already knew all about it."

In the fall of 1965 Ima Hogg moved out of Bayou Bend, and in March 1966 the house was opened to the public as the American Decorative Arts Wing of the Museum of Fine Arts. At eighty-three, Ima Hogg established herself in a new high-rise apartment at 3711 San Felipe Road.

At the end of the summer of 1975, Ima Hogg came back to Bayou Bend for the last time. The last few days of her life had been spent in a London hospital, where she had remained undaunted to the end. Uncomplaining after hours in a drafty emergency room, she was finally given an iron bed in a tiny boxlike cubicle open at the top — the nearest thing the hospital had to a private room. Facing surgery on her hip the day after the accident, she had dispatched Mrs. Coates to the hotel for her makeup case and demanded that her hair be combed. When Dr. William Lee Pryor, a close friend from Houston who had planned to meet her for a round of theatergoing in London, arrived distraught at the hospital, she had tried her best to cheer him. "Hold your shoulders up!" she had commanded. "I hardly recognized you." She had comforted Douglas McDugald, a favorite young cousin who had flown from Houston to be at her bedside. "It's all right," she had said. "I'm where I want to be."

On the afternoon of August 22, 1975, a private funeral service for Ima Hogg was held at Bayou Bend. As a sudden summer downpour drenched arriving mourners and pelted the neat rows of wooden folding chairs lined up in the garden, some 350 people crowded into the downstairs hall. Dripping wet, they dried their hands on paper towels before they signed the guest book. Standing on vinyl runners placed over the rare rugs, they tried not to brush against the eighteenth-century furniture. Those who came in first inched their way up the curving stairway to make room for the others. When there was no more space left, the latecomers, many bareheaded and without umbrellas, stood outside in the rain. Rich and poor, black and white, all stood in mute and solemn tribute to Miss Ima. There was Leon Jaworski, back from Watergate; he had been her attorney. There was Oscar Wilson, her yardman for twenty-three years; there was Gus Wortham, founder of the American General Insurance Company; there was Gertrude Vaughn, her maid for fifty-six years; there were the John Connallys, the Harris Mastersons, Oveta Culp Hobby, and the elite of Texas politics, art, and business. The University of Texas, her alma mater, declared two days of mourning and flew its flags at half-mast. With characteristic efficiency Ima Hogg had planned her funeral many years before her death, and had left meticulous and precise instructions for everything from the kind of flowers (magnolias) on the casket to the music—or rather, the absence of music. She had written: "I do not wish to subject my relatives to prolonged eulogies or ceremonies or to require them to listen to music which we so deeply loved and enjoyed during my lifetime." And so Ima Hogg, who had been passionately fond of music all her life, had none, by her own request, at her funeral. Instead, the Reverend Thomas Sumners, rector emeritus of St. John the Divine Episcopal Church, read from the Ninetieth Psalm, which ends:

"With my long life will I satisfy him /And show him my salvation."

Ima Hogg was buried in Austin's Oakwood Cemetery, on a tree-shaded hill in one of the oldest parts of the city. Her grave is next to those of her mother and father and her three brothers. That is as it should be, and as she wished it, for it was this family—especially her father—that Ima Hogg loved more than anything else.

2

A Texas Family

On a hot July day in 1882, the young district attorney for the Texas Seventh District sat in his office in Mineola and wrote a letter to his brother:

> Dear John —
>
> Our cup of joy is now overflowing! We have a daughter of as fine proportions and of as angelic mien as ever gracious nature favor a man with, and her name is Ima! Can't you come down to see her?
>
> She made her debut on last Monday night at 9 o'clock. Sallie is doing extremely well, and of course *Ima* is. — Next Saturday or Sunday I shall start for the State Convention at Galveston, as a Delegate from this Co. Would be glad to see you there.
>
> Love to Eva and the babes.
>
> Your Bro. —
> James

There is nothing unusual about this letter — except that the baby's last name happened to be Hogg. To this day there are some who believe that James Stephen Hogg, the bewhiskered, three-hundred-pound, six-foot-three giant of Texas politics, governor of the state from 1891 to 1895, named his only daughter Ima Hogg to attract the attention of Texas voters. (He was running for reelection in a close race for district attorney that year.) It is ironic that the founder of the Houston Symphony, the creator of the Bayou Bend Collection of the Museum of Fine Arts, the gracious and stately doyenne of Texas culture for several decades, was the daughter of a politician whose public image was seldom associated with refinement and whose reputation for earthy humor and populist rhetoric was as wide as his girth. To his daughter, however, James Stephen Hogg was a statesman

17

of the highest order, and she tried her best to carve out what she believed to be a proper niche for him in Texas history. She even had an explanation for the name he gave her.

According to Ima Hogg, her father named her for the heroine of *The Fate of Marvin*, a poem written in 1873 by his beloved elder brother, Thomas Elisha Hogg, who had died of typhoid two years before she was born. The brother, a Civil War veteran, had composed an epic about two brothers who fought on opposite sides in the conflict between the Blue and the Gray, and two sisters who married them. One of the sisters, Ima, is described as:

A Southern girl, whose winsome grace
And kindly, gentle mien, betrayed
A heart more beauteous than her face
Ah! she was fair: the Southern skies
Were typed in Ima's heavenly eyes.

In this epic, however, there are *two* Southern girls, and the other one is named Lelia. If all Jim Hogg wanted to do was name his little girl for a character in a family poem, he could have named her Lelia and spared her a lifetime of quizzical looks and crude jests about her name.

Ima Hogg herself allowed that at least one member of her family tried to register a protest — but he was not a Hogg. As she recalled the incident years later, "Grandfather Stinson lived fifteen miles from Mineola and news traveled slowly. When he learned of his granddaughter's name he came trotting to town as fast as he could to protest, but it was too late. The christening had taken place and Ima I was to remain."

Ima Hogg. No middle name, even in an era when middle names for little girls were almost as mandatory as lace on petticoats. Texas voters would not soon forget that Jim Hogg, for whom "portly" was an inadequate adjective and whose appearance on platforms was sometimes preceded by affectionate hogcalls from backwoods farmers, had named his daughter Ima. Hogg, who once began an acceptance speech for a nomination by saying, "I am one of those unfortunate animals from the pine-capped hills and persimmon valleys of East Texas that is not altogether a razor-back," was no fool when it came to name identification in politics.

With less strength of character Ima Hogg might have taken refuge in a nickname; with less family pride she would have changed the given name to something else. Instead, she carried it with a certain steely dignity and wry humor. In her memoirs of her childhood she wrote with some amusement that the family's cook had named her only daughter Ima, too, and that the "little colored Ima became a privileged character in our family." Looking back on those early years, Ima remembered how many times her older brother, Will, had come home from school with a bloody nose from defending, as she put it, "my good name." In Texas some people said that Ima Hogg had a sister named Ura and over the years other wags embellished the joke: Governor Hogg, they claimed, really had three daughters: Ima, Ura, and Shesa. Still others said that there were brothers named Hesa, Harry, and Moore. In Ima Hogg's personal papers there is a voluminous file of letters from people who wrote to her over the years, wanting to know if that really was her name, if she had a sister, and so on.

All her life Ima Hogg tried to disguise her name in a distinctive signature that rendered the first part almost illegible. Her personal stationery was printed "Miss Hogg" or sometimes "I. Hogg." In later years she tried whenever possible not to use her name at all. She would ask Jane Zivley, her secretary, to order items and make reservations under the name Zivley, not Hogg. In Houston, where she lived for nearly seventy years, and all over Texas, Ima Hogg became known as Miss Ima. Nobody except the rankest newcomer ever asked "Ima *who*?" On August 10, 1975, a few days before her death, the *New York Times* crossword clue for 36 across, a three-letter word, was "Miss Hogg."

Toward the end of her life Ima Hogg won what one close friend called "her victory over her name." A few months before her last trip to Europe in 1975 she remarked idly, "You know, if I had been born in Scotland, my name would probably have been Imogene." Not long afterward, she began to call herself Imogene. The whimsical name change was a well-kept secret. Even some of the people closest to her never knew it, but her last passport was issued to Ima Imogene Hogg. At her friend William Lee Pryor's house in Houston is an oak-framed photograph she gave him the summer before her death. It is Ima Hogg as a turn-of-the-century belle, a pretty, thoughtful-looking young lady in white lace and ruffles. The picture is inscribed, "To Lee Pryor, from Imogene with love."

Perhaps more than anything else it was Ima Hogg's idolization of the man who named her that made her keep the name for most of her ninety-three years. James Stephen Hogg was a man whose ponderous physical stature and prodigious political appetites made him one of the most colorful and controversial figures in Texas political history. Ebullient and supremely self-confident, he had come up the hard way, by his own efforts, and if he pleased to call his daughter Ima Hogg there was not much anybody could do about it.

Jim Hogg was not the first of the Hoggs to enter the political arena. His grandfather Thomas Hogg was elected to the Georgia legislature in 1814, the Alabama legislature in 1819, and the Mississippi legislature in 1836, as the Hoggs, like many a Southern family in the years before the Civil War, migrated westward in search of economic opportunity. Thomas Hogg found his, and died a wealthy and respected planter-lawyer in Bellefontaine, Mississippi, in 1849. His son, Joseph Lewis Hogg, born in Georgia in 1806, continued the family tradition by serving in the legislature of the young Republic of Texas when he moved there in 1839, and in 1845, when the Lone Star Republic became the twenty-eighth state, he helped write the new state constitution.

Texas in those days was the Texas of countless Western movies: a raw frontier where hostile Indians still prowled, white men wore guns, and acres of fertile land lay waiting for the plow. Joseph Lewis Hogg settled his family — his young wife, Lucanda, and their two daughters, Martha Frances, age five, and Julia Ann, not yet a year old, on a plantation on Loco Creek near Nacogdoches. There, in 1842, the first son, Thomas Elisha, was born. Hogg left them in 1845 to serve with the Second Texas Regiment in the Mexican War, and when he returned the family moved once again, to a site near Rusk, the seat of newly created Cherokee County. There, at "Mountain Home," in the gently rolling hills of East Texas, Colonel Hogg planted cotton, practiced law, and added more acres to his holdings. By the time the Civil War broke out, Hogg would have 2,500 acres. In 1848 another son, John Washington, was added to the Hogg household, and in 1851, James Stephen was born. Two more boys, Joseph Lewis, Jr., born in 1854, and Richard, born in 1856, made Mountain Home a full house, indeed. It was a busy house as well, bustling with preparations for an incessant stream of visitors — the Hoggs knew how to dispense Southern hospitality — and filled with the commotion that seven children and assorted house servants could create. The Hoggs, like other planter families, were slaveowners, and when the Civil War came they owned twenty. Colonel Joseph Lewis Hogg, tall and stern-faced, brooked no nonsense from his children, and one may be fairly certain that he was equally demanding of his slaves. He liked to see the proprieties observed, and he seems to have had pretensions to greatness. He once bought high silk hats for his elder sons and insisted they wear them to school. The remarks of their classmates are not recorded, but they are not beyond imagining, and they ended only when Tom, the eldest, finally rebelled and demolished his hat in protest. Perhaps that episode was an object lesson to his little brother James Stephen, who in later life made unpretentiousness part of his political stock-in-trade.

James Stephen Hogg was ten years old when the Confederate guns shelled Fort Sumter, and his life, like many another, was to be forever changed by what followed. His father, who had been an ardent secessionist (differing with his longtime friend, Sam Houston, who had to step down as governor in 1860 when Texas voted to accept the Ordinance of Secession), was given the rank of brigadier general by the new governor, former lieutenant governor Edward Clark. Hogg was assigned the task of recruiting and training soldiers in Texas' Fifth Military District to help meet the state's quota of eight thousand men for the Confederate forces. In the spring of 1862 General Joseph Lewis Hogg was called to active duty and given a Confederate command. He joined his troops in Tennessee, just after the battle of Shiloh in April 1862. Five weeks later, near Corinth, Mississippi, before he could order out so much as a single platoon in battle, he was dead of dysentery. Thirty years later, his son James Stephen, then governor of Texas, would commission a portrait of him in his Confederate uniform and hang it in the Governor's Mansion, and more than half a century after that, his granddaughter Ima would hang that portrait of him in the Texas Room at Bayou Bend.

There were sad times at Mountain Home after General Hogg's death. At home, besides the younger children — Richard, six; Joseph, Jr., eight; James, ten; and John, twelve — there were twenty-three-year-old Julia (whose husband-to-be, Dr. William McDugald, was in the war as well) and Martha Frances, now twenty-eight and the widowed mother of a son, William, nearly the same age as his cousin James. Her young husband, William Davis, had died of consumption in 1851. Tom, the Hoggs' eldest son, who had left college at nineteen to enlist when the war broke out and would see it end as a captain in Confederate gray, was with his father at the time of his death. Young "Marse Tom" came home in the fall of 1862 to comfort the family and help get in that year's cotton crop.

There was mourning that year not only for General Hogg but also for a Major James Barker, killed in battle near Corinth. He had been courting the widowed Martha Frances Davis, and after his death she devoted her life to mothering the various children of the Hogg family as well as her own son. It was Martha Frances — "Sister Frank" — who had to take over as head of the household the very next summer when Richard, the youngest of the Hogg brood, and their mother, Lucanda McMath Hogg, became ill and died within a few days of each other.

Ima Hogg

It was Martha Frances who comforted young James Stephen Hogg after the death of his father, brother, and mother; and it would be Martha Frances, more than thirty years later, who would comfort him and his children after the death of his wife.

For the duration of the war, Mountain Home, which had once echoed with the laughter and noise of a happy family, was a quieter place. The two young women and five little boys waited as the war news worsened and their holdings dwindled. Some of the land had been sold, and an 1864 inventory listed only six slaves. (Emancipation did not come to Texas until after the war's end, when on June 19, 1865, a Yankee general in Galveston proclaimed the state to be once again part of the United States, with all former slaves freed. "Juneteenth" has been a special day of celebration for blacks in Texas ever since.) Tom Hogg married not long after the war ended, as did his sister Julia, but the family fortunes failed to improve, and Reconstruction brought falling land values and financially precarious times.

Young Jim Hogg went to work as a printer's devil for the Rusk newspaper, the *Texas Observer*, in 1867. He was sixteen. For the next few years he learned the newspaper business, working for the *Palestine Advocate*, the *Cleburne Chronicle*, the *Quitman Clipper*, and the *Tyler Democrat-Reporter*, whose editor wrote this description of the nineteen-year-old Hogg many years later:

> He was large of limb and physically well developed, but rather awkward, not very well educated, not particularly handsome, as poor as Job's turkey, and by no means a dude. We liked his looks, nevertheless, and gave him a job. . . . His leisure hours (and he had not many) were assiduously devoted to study, and many a time, while he had a home within our family circle, midnight found him bending over his books; and with only a few hours' sleep each night, the dawn of day found him again plodding his unaided and slow, but sure way along the paths of knowledge.

A generation earlier, the same piece could have been written about another young frontier lad named Abraham Lincoln. This sketch of Jim Hogg, written in 1886 during his campaign for state attorney general, reveals how pervasive the poor-boy-makes-good myth had become in American politics.

Jim Hogg's early struggles were not all myth, by any means, and before he was twenty he had tried his hand as a sharecropper, worked in a cotton gin, and leased a small patch of farmland with his brother

A Texas Family

John. Once, broke and traveling from Cleburne to Rusk, he went three days without food. In 1869, while he was working near Quitman, he was shot in the back by an outlaw and lay near death for several weeks. The shooting was the result of a brush with the gang of outlaws the year before, when five of them had tried to kill the local sheriff. Young Hogg and a friend "got the drop on them," as Hogg explained this incident years later, and the "desperadoes" surrendered — vowing to get revenge. Texas, even after the Civil War, was still a frontier area, and shoot-outs, even in East Texas, were common. Hogg's father, Joseph Lewis Hogg, had been shot and severely wounded by a young man in Rusk, and then had later killed his adversary in a shoot-out on the town square in 1850.

Young Jim Hogg, recovering from his wounds at Mountain Home in 1869 (all that remained was the house and 530 acres of the original 2,500-acre plantation), had some time to think. What he thought of mostly was his boyhood dream of becoming a lawyer. No doubt he also thought of a petite dark-haired young lady with gray eyes named Sallie Stinson, whom he had met in 1869 during his brief time at Mr. Baggett's School near Quitman. But Sallie was the daughter of a prosperous sawmill owner, and Jim Hogg was a penniless young man with few prospects.

At last he decided to go back to the newspaper business, especially since the bullet lodged near his spine would now prevent him from doing heavy farm work. One of his father's friends in Rusk allowed him to use his law library during his convalescence, and then a job on the *Tyler Democrat-Reporter* put Jim Hogg back in the world of printing and politics — a world he found increasingly to his liking. By 1871 he had decided to strike out on his own, and he started his own newspaper, the *Longview News*. For a time, James S. Hogg, Publisher, not only wrote the copy and set the type but ran the presses, distributed the paper, swapped advertising space for groceries, and slept in his office. The paper prospered, and the next year, Hogg moved his operation to Quitman, where the paper became the *Quitman News*. Although financial opportunity was the reason for the move, the fact that Sallie Stinson lived a few miles outside Quitman was no doubt an added attraction. The hardworking young editor-publisher now studied law on his own and talked politics with his friends. Texas after Reconstruction was an exciting place to do that. There was heady talk of railroad expansion and business opportunities in a state where the population had already grown from about 40,000 in the 1830s to over 800,000 by the 1870s. There was also exciting talk about the political future now that Republican influence

Ima Hogg

was on the wane. In 1873, at the age of twenty-two, Jim Hogg entered politics and won his first election as justice of the peace of Wood County, Texas. Political ambition had not kept him from courting Sallie Stinson, however, and on April 22, 1874, the two were married at the Stinson home near Quitman.

The newlyweds settled into their first home, a tiny four-room frame house. In January 1875 their first child, William Clifford, was born, and in the spring Jim Hogg, who had read law on his own for several years, was finally admitted to practice before the Texas bar. In 1876 the aspiring young politician, then twenty-five, ran for the Texas legislature from the Twenty-second District, but he did not win. It was the only political race he ever lost. Hogg did not give up, and two years later, in 1878, he ran for office again. Campaigning on a slogan of "Enforce the Law" (natives of Wood County still refer to certain liquid measures as Jim Hogg quarts in memory of Hogg's crusade against short measures in kerosene and whiskey), Hogg was elected to the office of county attorney. In 1880 he was elected district attorney for the Texas Seventh District. In 1886, when his daughter Ima was four years old, he was elected attorney general of the state of Texas, and in 1890 James Stephen Hogg won the governorship.

In the meantime two more children had been added to the Hogg household: Michael, born in 1885, and Thomas Elisha, born in 1887. Attorney General Hogg had moved his family to Austin (then a town of some 14,000 people) in December 1886. There they could watch the building of the massive new state capitol building, which was finished in 1888. The family lived for a time at the Andrews boardinghouse at the corner of Eleventh and Lavaca streets before buying a two-story house on Fourteenth Street.

These moves took their toll on Sallie Hogg, who was pregnant with Tom, and after his birth in August 1887 she never quite regained her strength. For a time the new baby was cared for by a black wet nurse who fed him along with her own infant son, but when the Hogg family moved into the white-columned Governor's Mansion in January 1891 Sallie was still not in good health. Ima remembered her mother in those years as having "fair skin, with not much color." Sallie Hogg was not one to complain, however, and she set about refurbishing the somewhat dilapidated old Governor's Mansion, directing painters and carpenters, replacing some of the worn furniture in the parlors and library with new rattan pieces, and modernizing the one bathroom with its enormous tin tub that had been installed in the 1850s for Sam Houston. Her daughter's later comments about her reveal something of Sallie Stinson Hogg's quiet strength: "She was, more than anything else, a homemaker in every sense of the word. She encouraged and believed in my father's career, but she was a very shy person and shrank from all public appearances herself." But Ima remembered how Sallie Hogg, exquisitely gowned, was at her husband's side for innumerable receptions in the Governor's Mansion—even when her frail strength gave out and she had to sit or lean against a high stool. Sallie was a meticulous housekeeper and directed every detail of these endless entertainments, often giving orders to the servants from her bed. "She loved to make her home one of charm and hospitality," her daughter recalled. "Our only income was my father's salary, which was not large; so my mother had to be thrifty and wise in her expenditures, and yet she always managed to give an atmosphere of bountiful living."

For her family and a constant stream of visitors, the ailing Sallie Hogg kept up appearances in the Governor's Mansion, presiding over a household that was, to say the least, seldom peaceful or quiet. With four children—Will, fifteen; Ima, eight; Mike, five; and Tom, three— and assorted dogs, cats, and other pets, including a Shetland pony and a parrot that cried, "Papa! Papa!" when the governor came home, the house near the capitol was livelier than it had been in many a year. As Ima remarked years later, "I am afraid visitors to the mansion must have thought we were a pretty rowdy trio, Mike, Tom, and myself." She recalled that Will considered himself too old for childish pranks—"of course, Brother was dignified and not often conspicuous"—but she and her younger brothers were fond of sliding down the stair railings: "We three would start at the top of the steps and slide down one after the other with a great thud into the center hall." Their indulgent father, who never resorted to corporal punishment, took other action after little Tom cut his chin sliding down that banister: "Father then took tacks and hammered them all the way down the railing of the stairs." The holes in the polished oak were visible for many years, and were pointed out to visitors to the historic governor's house. Governor Hogg was also annoyed at having to have the fence palings constantly repaired because his younger children kept removing parts of the fence to make it easier for their friends to crawl through. On one occasion, so a family story goes, Tom tried to solve this problem by burning down the fence.

Sallie Hogg did what she could to keep her rambunctious brood in order, insisting, for example, that the tomboy Ima learn needlework, but her daughter "never had the patience to succeed." The children's mother also tried other tactics: "Mother had a little switch which she would use on our legs sometimes." Governor Hogg would regularly lend a hand by taking all the children for a long Sunday afternoon drive to give his wife some peace and quiet. The children's antics seem not to have bothered their father when he was at home. He was a great reader in his leisure hours, and as Ima remembered, his "powers of concentration were astonishing. We were very noisy, undisciplined children and no amount of noisy or boisterous behavior around the house ever seemed to disturb him." The children were encouraged to read, too, and Ima remembered reading the works of James Fenimore Cooper and Nathaniel Hawthorne as well as "all the Alcott stories." The children's mother wanted them to learn languages, and for a time they had a German housemaid who served as a sort of governess for the younger children. Although their lessons were in English, Ima recalled that "we said our prayers in German at her knee." Sallie Hogg saw to it that Ima continued her studies with a Mrs. Ziller, a German woman who ran a kindergarten in Austin. The children's cultural life was not neglected, either, and Ima remembered being taken to the Millet Opera House in Austin to see Shakespeare productions and performances by traveling opera companies.

On Sunday mornings the three younger children attended Sunday school at the Methodist Church on Tenth Street, while the governor and his frail wife remained at home. James Stephen Hogg was a religious man, but never a regular churchgoer. He was fond of singing hymns, however, and on Sunday nights the parlor piano in the Governor's Mansion was put to use in a hymn-sing for family and friends. Ima often played, and Sallie too, when she felt strong enough. It was Sallie, in fact, who had been Ima's first music teacher.

Will Hogg by this time was enrolled as a student at Southwestern University in nearby Georgetown. Sallie, whose father was a lay preacher in the Methodist church, hoped that Will would become a minister. Will, then in his teens, seems to have been his mother's special favorite. The governor was busy with affairs of state; the younger children were a rowdy crew; and so it was often Will whom Sallie Hogg took on her excursions to shops and dressmakers. Will, his sister recalled, always liked clothes, which, she said, "I think accounted for his later very fastidious taste. He knew as much as any woman about materials and appropriate dressing."

In the years in the Governor's Mansion, Will did not join in the frolics of his younger siblings. He was, after all, as Ima said later, "nearly nine years older than I and always seemed a young man to me." She was much closer in age and spirit to her younger brothers: "We were very energetic children and played out of doors a great deal." Tom was "very sweet and affectionate"; Mike was "witty and tormentor." Governor Hogg nicknamed Mike the Yellow Kid after a mischievous character in one of the first newspaper comic strips. Ima and the boys were inseparable companions in those years, playing games with their friends on the spacious grounds of the Governor's Mansion ("I was allowed to compete with the boys," she said) and riding or driving their Shetland pony, Dainty, around the grounds. The pony did not always cooperate, and according to Ima the children were "often pitched to the ground."

The governor left the mansion every morning at eight to walk to his office at the Capitol, came home at midday for the noon meal and a nap, and then went back to work until dusk, but he tried to spend as much time as he could with his family. When the circus came to town he always took his own and neighboring children, and afterward, said Ima, "for days . . . we children went through all sorts of contortions, trying to practice some of the acts of the acrobats," which made her mother fearful, but "Father would look on and applaud."

In the summers the children spent part of their time at the country home of the Stinsons, Sallie's parents, in East Texas near Mineola. One of Ima Hogg's earliest surviving letters was written from her grandparents' home the summer before her father was elected governor. The seven-year-old Ima told her father that she had "picked 4 pounds of cotton" and that she "weighed 51 pounds today." At the end of the letter she wrote, "I wood like to know what you and Brother are doing."

These visits to East Texas made a lasting impression on her, and years later she described them in some detail in her memoirs. The families on small farms near the prosperous Stinson spread made a particularly vivid impression. "I wondered at the lack of comfort and ambition among them," she wrote. Compared to the bounty at her grandfather's house, where the table was always set with an extra place or two for guests who might drop by, the Stinsons' neighbors, Ima thought, lived a meager life indeed. She was shocked that they had little in their gardens but potatoes and cabbages, and that they seemed to eat an unvarying diet of salt pork, cornbread, and molasses, with occasional side dishes of black-eyed peas or sweet potatoes. The women went barefoot, and "some of the children in the families had hare-lips and I am quite sure many of them had hook worm." But what disturbed her most was that they all seemed content with their lot, and were "utterly without ambition" — something that Ima Hogg would never be.

Looking back on her summers at the Stinsons', she wrote fondly of her grandfather's widowed oldest sister, Lizzie Phillips, whose room she shared. Aunt Lizzie was "quite thin and old," but "merry." She was not too old, however, to play duets with Ima on the piano and ride a horse to visit the neighbors, with Ima perched on the saddle behind her. It may have been Aunt Lizzie who first inspired Ima Hogg's lifelong interest in antiques. In their bedroom at the Stinson house was a handsome old bureau that had belonged to Ima's great-grandmother, and Lizzie, Ima recalled, pointed it out to her with the promise that "some day it would be mine." It was, indeed, and the bureau now graces a bedroom of the house at the Varner plantation, the former Hogg home given by Ima Hogg to the State of Texas as Varner-Hogg Plantation State Park, near West Columbia.

Some of Ima Hogg's fascination with historic preservation and antiques also came from her memories of life in the antebellum Governor's Mansion in Austin, where she was allowed to sleep in Sam Houston's massive four-poster bed. The house itself had been built for Governor Sam Houston in 1855. The Greek Revival structure had housed eleven Texas governors since then, but James Stephen Hogg was the first native-born Texan to occupy it. When Ima Hogg was ninety-two, an interviewer for an oral history project asked her what life had been like in the Governor's Mansion, and she replied with a wry laugh, "Horrible, horrible! The ceilings were seventeen feet high; no heat, just little iron grates you put coal in. We had colds all the time. It was dreadful. And the bathtub was at the end of the house in an ell. It was put there by Sam Houston. About eight feet long, and you had to pump water into it. Very primitive. Very, very primitive! We enjoyed living there, though, because Father was very social, and he had a lot of receptions, and he had a lot of guests."

Ima, who had been playing the piano since the age of three, often played for her doting father and his company. On such occasions, as she recalled, her "childish efforts on the piano and banjo were in frequent demand." But there was a somber side to life in the Governor's Mansion, the shadow of Sallie Hogg's frail health: "Mother was quite ill. She was an invalid, really. I don't know how she did what she did—how she kept house, and had guests, and everything. And nobody knew what was the matter with her. They thought she had stomach trouble."

Sallie Hogg had tuberculosis, but it was not diagnosed until Hogg left office in 1895. In the meantime, as Sallie's condition worsened, the anxious governor thought a change of scene and some time at health spas might be beneficial. "Father sent us to Arkansas, and to every resort in Texas. I went with her, and I slept with her. It's a wonder I didn't contract it, isn't it? You'd think I would. I went with my mother everywhere, when she went off to those resorts. I slept with her. They didn't have a decent hotel in Texas."

When Sallie Hogg's illness was finally identified, the doctor recommended that she go to Colorado. By a stroke of good fortune, Martha Frances Davis, Jim Hogg's widowed older sister, was then living in Pueblo, Colorado. Her only son, William, now a physician, had found his own case of tuberculosis arrested by the dry Colorado air. Ima and her mother went to stay with the Davises, and for a while hopes for Sallie's recovery rose. Ex-governor Hogg and the boys, however, remained in Austin during that summer. One reason for this may have been financial. Sallie's travels and medical care must have depleted her husband's financial resources. Ima remembered that her father "left the mansion in great debt and it was quite necessary for him to immediately make connections which would establish him in law practice."

Late in August, word came from Pueblo that Sallie's strength had begun to fail. Husband and sons hurried to join Ima at the bedside, and on September 20, 1895, Sallie Stinson Hogg died. Ima, just thirteen that summer, had been with her mother through it all. The death of a loved one is traumatic at any age, and the death of a mother from a dread disease, for a sensitive adolescent, must have been especially painful. Her mother's death undoubtedly left its mark on Ima Hogg, but she could not — or perhaps would not — speak of it later in her reminiscences of that time in her life. Her account of her mother's death in her memoirs is limited to two strangely emotionless sentences: "She was young and optimistic, and I am sure no one ever dreamed that she would not recover. Her remains were brought back to Austin and with us came my father's oldest sister, Martha Frances Davis."

Unlike his daughter, James Stephen Hogg was able to articulate his grief. Nearly a month after his wife's death, he wrote to his sister Julia:

> In all the storms of an eventful life the severest shock that I ever received was the death of poor Sallie. Indeed, since Mother's death when I was twelve, I had never been called to witness the death of a relative. It is all over except now and then — almost hourly — when memory recalls the past and with it my wife's suffering and death compared to her gentleness and virtues. Then my feelings overcome me. She never spoke an unkind word to me in her life and never had I to account to others for a word or act of hers. God knows if all men were so blessed the earth would be more like heaven. My ambition is to

Ima Hogg

raise my children after her model. If I succeed the world will be much better for it.

The bereaved father had someone to lend a hand with the children: his sister Martha Frances, "Aunt Fannie," who had come to Austin with the Hoggs for Sallie's funeral and stayed on. But the adjustment to life without their mother must have been difficult for the Hogg children, and life with them was obviously not easy for Martha Frances Davis. "Aunt Fannie," Ima observed, "was not prepared by experience or nature to have charge of such undisciplined children as she found us to be." She "believed in giving us chores and filling every idle moment when we were out of school, with some duties." Reading aloud to them from Plutarch's *Lives* and "juvenile versions of the lives of heroes," this paragon of virtue meant well but "served mainly to make the children unhappy." Later in 1895 their father decided to send the three younger children, Ima, then thirteen, and Mike, ten, and Tom, eight, away to boarding school at the Coronal Institute in nearby San Marcos. Will, then twenty, was in Austin studying for a career in law at the University of Texas.

The next year, in 1896, Jim Hogg bought a big two-and-a-half-story house on the corner of Nineteenth and Rio Grande streets, where the children were able to resume a more or less normal routine, and where they began to collect a menagerie of pets. Besides the usual assortment of hunting dogs, there were at various times a horse, a bear, a fawn, and two ostriches named Jack and Jill. The children's father did his part to add to this collection. In San Antonio, seeing an exhibit of birds, he bought an entire cage of cockatoos. On a hunting trip he wounded a wild goose that he brought home and named Polly. The bird became very fond of him, and some years later, as Ima wrote, Polly "died at the same hour that he did. We always thought this was an interesting coincidence." In the house on Rio Grande, Ima fondly recalled, "we entered upon an era of very simple domestic life with Father acting as provider, father and mother all together to his little family."

Jim Hogg tried to give his children a good upbringing. To Will, then a rather solemn young man in his twenties, Hogg laid down some rules for living: "Be a good boy. Take care of yourself. Exercise freely. Sweat often and profusely. Drink plenty of good water. Do most of your work in daytime. Sleep at night. Treat all people honorably and politely. Do not overlook small things except such as fret you." Will, by this time, was finishing his work at the University of Texas law school, where he graduated in 1897. Ex-governor Hogg, busy with his own law practice, still found time to spend with his eldest son, and when the Spanish-American War broke out in 1898, both father and son wanted to enlist. Jim Hogg, at age forty-seven and weighing 275 pounds, could not pass the physical; Will, waiting for a commission in the Navy, never got in, either.

Meanwhile, Ima, at sixteen, had had to take over as "lady of the house." The Hoggs had engaged a housekeeper after Aunt Fannie's departure, but domestic responsibilities fell heavily upon Ima. Her aunt's letters to her are filled with housecleaning hints ("Take one room at a time") and suggestions for Mike's and Tom's reading. In one letter Aunt Fannie exhorted Ima to spend more time with her younger brothers in their studies: "They are great big boys and they will need all the help they can get." The help, in Aunt Fannie's estimation, should come from their older sister's listening to them read aloud. She suggested a daily plan whereby each of the boys would read for one hour, with Ima as audience. This, she said, would of course take up two hours of Ima's time every day, but it would be time well spent. Whether the sixteen-year-old Ima found time to follow all her aunt's instructions is not known, but she wrote of this period later that Mike and Tom, "being very lively, mischievous little boys, got along rather poorly in public school."

Not long after her mother's death, Ima Hogg's well-meaning but misinformed Aunt Fannie told her that she must never marry, because she would be a carrier of tuberculosis. Martha Frances Davis had good reason to fear the disease: it was one of the most common causes of death in the nineteenth century, and she remembered all too vividly how her husband, Will Davis, had died of consumption before their son was born in 1852, and how that son had himself contracted tuberculosis as a young man. Ima, thus bound by turn-of-the-century medical lore, was to devote the next eighty years to the pursuit of interests other than matrimony. It was not, however, that she herself was not pursued. In 1899, as a coed at the University of Texas, with blonde hair piled high, vivid blue eyes, and a petite figure dressed in as stylish a manner as an indulgent father's income would allow, Ima Hogg at the turn of the century might have posed as a model for one of Charles Dana Gibson's drawings. Many years later, a college friend, Gretchen Rochs Goldschmidt (class of 1903), reminisced about Governor Hogg's daughter in a sketch for the *Alcalde*, the alumni magazine of the University of Texas:

> Can you see a young lady riding across the capitol grounds? What a picture of grace, skill, beauty, and horsemanship! The

Ima Hogg

black close-fitting riding-habit that only a woman of superb physique could carry off to perfection, the shining beaver with its fluttering veil . . . the gauntlets, the riding-crop, the long sweep of the robe over the feet; the erect and of necessity a bit unnatural carriage in the side-saddle, all this is now as extinct as the Dinosaur: still none of those who saw the golden-haired Amazon of that time can forget the stately beauty and the thrill of it.

Ima Hogg, unapproachable as she appeared seen atop the gallant steed, was in reality a charming freshman, unaffected in manner and a most conscientious student. . . .

There were happy times at the house on Rio Grande, when young lawyer Will entertained his friends, and when Ima's beaux came to call. Sixty-five years later, an elderly man hailed Ima Hogg, then in her eighties, in an art gallery in Phoenix, Arizona: "Ima Hogg, isn't it? I remember you! I was a Kappa Alpha at the university when you were there. I remember how, when a fellow wanted to come courting you, the whole fraternity had to come along to keep your little brothers out of the way. They used to hide under the porch and turn the hose on us!"

Perhaps the greatest rival for Ima's affections in those days, however, was her doting father. Fiercely proud of her, he almost hated to see her grow up. A few months before her seventeenth birthday, while he was away on business, he sent her a letter written by his nephew, Francis Baylor Hogg, who had remarked that he found Ima "unassuming modest sweet and pretty. Ima is an exceptional girl. . . . She is now just budding into womanhood—a sweeter girl is not to be found." Jim Hogg marked this passage with a note to Ima: "Now don't let this spoil you." On her birthday that same year he wrote to her: "Today I have been reflecting—*you are seventeen years old!* If on this account you are *weaned* I am sorry for it. But I am not weaned from you. In every feature of your face, in every movement of your hand I can see your Mother. Perhaps this of all other causes accounts for my partiality for you. . . . In you I look for a friend and counsellor as wise, as faithful, as true."

For the rest of his life, until his death in 1906, James Stephen Hogg's affections were centered on his only daughter, and afterward, she, in turn, was to devote much of her own long life to the preservation of his memory and the enhancement of his place in Texas history.

3

The Governor's Daughter

James Stephen Hogg entered politics at a time when the Populist, or People's, party of the 1890s was clamoring for legislation to protect the little man from big business, and the political arena was more exciting than it had been since the Age of Jackson. It was the era of "Pitchfork Ben" Tillman and Mary Elizabeth "Raise Less Corn and More Hell" Lease. Politics itself was more of a spectator sport in those days — perhaps filling a need now satisfied by professional athletics. It was the age of open-air rallies and torchlight parades and box-supper meetings; of long-winded speeches and hard-fought campaigns. Popular political candidates in the late nineteenth century were attended with as much hoopla as rock stars are in the twentieth.

Jim Hogg was not a Populist, he was a Democrat — but he ran on a reform ticket, and his tirades against the "wildcat" insurance companies and the railroads that controlled some forty million acres of Texas land made him the natural target of conservative interests and corporate wealth. The gargantuan governor gloried in his grass-roots strength, and on the campaign trail he played to the crowds. His initial campaign speech in Rusk, Texas, on April 19, 1890, lasted nearly three hours, and the crowd hung on every word. "Mill around," he would say to his overalled audience, "and skin out if you get tired." They never did. "I *know* the common people are with me," he once told a sweating, cheering crowd on a hot summer afternoon, "because I can *smell* 'em!"

Politics was meat and drink to Jim Hogg in those days. In mid-July of the gubernatorial campaign of 1890, his sister Martha Frances wrote to him, "William says you are a goner into politics — that it is too fascinating for a man to pull out easily." He did not pull out. Campaigning for a second term as governor in 1892, sometimes with a gingham-dressed Ima on his knee, Hogg ran against another Democrat, a Waco lawyer named George W. Clark, in one of the bitterest

33

and most violent contests in the history of the state. It was a grueling campaign that left the governor little time for his family. When Sallie and the children left Austin to visit the Stinson grandparents in East Texas, Hogg wrote a plaintive letter from the empty Governor's Mansion in Austin: "Have a nice time and enjoy yourselves. . . . I'll be there I hope by watermelon time. Then we will all go fishing and have a big frolic. Around the house here from morning 'till night there's not a sound of a rat, cat, or cricket. The cow, parrots, the dogs, all are gone. I am like a ghost in a two-story barn deserted." But he needed all the time to himself he could get, to plan his strategy in the struggle against what he considered evil forces.

Hogg's first term as governor had seen the enactment of Texas' first antitrust legislation and the establishment of the Railroad Commission, and he continued to rail against corrupt corporate power and to seek his support from the country folks, the "boys from the forks of the creek." Hogg's opponent, Clark, claimed that the governor's regulatory measures were driving investment capital out of the state and campaigned with the slogan "Turn Texas Loose!" One of his best campaign posters featured a comely young woman whose dress was being chewed by a large hog. There was a long poem underneath which read in part: "Save me from the snares of Hogg! / Save me from the demagogue!" (This cartoon, popular as it was, is not among those reproduced in the Ima Hogg–approved biography of James Stephen Hogg, published in 1959.)

Neither the Clark nor the Hogg faction of the Democratic party ever let the voters forget that the candidate who claimed to represent the rural folk against the city slickers and big business (and who weighed close to three hundred pounds) was named Hogg. The governor's supporters carried banners that read, "We Love Hogg for His Grit," "Don't Loosen the Belly Band," and "We Do Business at the Forks." Hogg's enemies found such imagery irresistible: "Hogg has rooted in the public pastures long enough, turn him out," said the *Navasota Leader*, a Clark paper. "Hogg is not making any stir at present. He is laying low and preparing for his rush from the thicket next week. There will be no doubt about his coming out with his bristles set and his back up," said the *San Antonio Light*.

Ima Hogg was ten years old in the summer of 1892, and her father often took her with him on the campaign trail. On June 14, 1892, the *Dallas Morning News* commented on what good use "the Governor and his little daughter" were making of Hogg's railroad pass that summer. Sallie Hogg's frail health and the care of the younger children took her out of the race, but Jim Hogg and his only daughter were a guaranteed crowd-pleaser in the hustings. Old-timers in Texas still tell stories about how Hogg used to appear with Ima and often a friend or two of hers, dressed in gingham and sitting on the back of a buckboard or on the campaign platform, and how sometimes he would introduce the little girls to his audience: "This is Ima Hogg, and this is Ura Hogg . . ." as the crowd roared with delight. (That, so the story goes, is how the myth of Hogg's other daughters named Ura and Shesa got started — but Ima always denied that such scenes ever took place.) In one of the scrapbooks in the Hogg papers at the University of Texas in an undated, unidentified newspaper clipping: "Governor Hogg of Texas has three bright children, two girls and a boy, whose names respectfully are said to be Ima Hogg, Ura Hogg, and Moore Hogg. These names were bestowed by Governor Hogg himself." Pasting his scrapbooks (she may, in fact, have pasted that clipping) and listening to his speeches, the governor's daughter was his most devoted supporter, and after his death, his most ardent defender. Sometimes she had her work cut out for her.

As the summer of 1892 wore on, feelings in the Hogg and Clark camps ran as high as the June and July temperatures. Fistfights, not unknown in Texas politics, broke out more often than ever at rallies and parades. At a joint debate in Cleburne, where thousands gathered to cheer their respective candidates, the crowds made so much noise that neither Hogg's nor Clark's speech could be heard, and a section of bleachers collapsed with two thousand people, injuring twenty. Each side began to accuse the other of rigging the county conventions. From the newspapers, most of which were for Clark, it is next to impossible to tell what really went on, and young Ima Hogg, working on her father's scrapbooks, must have had difficulty at times finding something good to put in.

"It seems impossible for a Hogg man to be a candidate for any position without the adoption by his supporters of a system of bulldozing and ruffianism," fumed the *Waco Globe.* "The Hogg and Clark campaign now drawing to a close has been the dirtiest and most disgraceful in the history of the state," said the *Comanche Chief.* "Can Texas afford to respect a nomination that was secured by undemocratic methods and the grossest frauds ever perpetuated upon the ballot boxes in the state? . . . Hogg must not be the next governor of this State!" said the *Texas Iconoclast.* These clippings are not among those in the Hogg scrapbooks that Ima kept at Bayou Bend.

Ima's childish reactions to the criticisms of her father are not recorded, but she did comment later on her parents' response: "Mother was very sensitive and suffered a great deal over campaign stories derogatory to Father. Of course, Father tried to make light of all such things no matter how he may have felt, but she never could see them that way."

On the other hand, those who were for Hogg were convinced that he could do no wrong. Said the *Corsicana Light*: "Governor Hogg represents the only true democracy there is in Texas at this time." The *Terrell Times-Star* had this to say:

A man never made a more magnificent fight nor none a more triumphant victory than Hogg has this year. All the corporations against him; all the daily papers against him; three-fourths of the lawyers against him; the life insurance companies against him; the fire insurance companies against him; the town lot boomers against him, the land sharks against him; the railroads against him; and yet he has triumphed. His friends have stuck to him like a brother and have been abused for his sake. . . . The common people have been his friends and they know he has been theirs. It is a triumph that any man may well feel proud of.

As the state convention in Houston in August approached, the Hogg and Clark forces prepared for a battle for the Democratic party's nomination, and some even packed their guns. Houston was ready for them. A bustling town of 27,000 people in 1890, it was not yet as large as Dallas or Galveston, but by 1900 it would outstrip both of them. In 1891 it had installed streetcars, and the new car barn owned by the Houston City Street Railway Company was to be the site of the convention. The barn had been specially fitted with seats to accommodate eight thousand delegates and spectators. "Best of all," crowed the *Houston Daily Post*, "over the heads of these devoted democrats will buzz and whirr, will breathe and blow thirty-five of the largest and latest kind of electric fans. This is a new method of cooling partisan ardor." Fans did little good, however, against the tempers that flared as Hogg and Clark men, each accusing the other of trying to pack the convention, confronted each other in arguments on the platform and in fistfights on the floor. The Clark forces finally left, dubbed "Boltercrats" by the triumphant Jim Hogg. The Democratic party in Texas was hopelessly split that year, but in the end Hogg won handily over Clark and the Populist candidate, Thomas L. Nugent. In November, when the election returns were in, the *Houston Daily Post* cartoon showed a porcine Hogg with walruslike whiskers swallowing a frock-coated figure labeled "Clark."

Even the *Daily Post*, the only major newspaper in the state that supported Hogg, could not resist the ready-made humor in a three-hundred-pound candidate named Hogg. During the party convention the paper ran a tongue-in-cheek account of Hogg in his headquarters in the Capitol Hotel: "The governor was dressed en dishabille with his shirt and pants worn decollete and his half hose of Prussian black tipped with Alaska white cunningly playing peek-a-boo with the wrinkled bed spread." The *Post* also reported that "at 6:30 precisely a startling sound like the last expiring gasp of an asthmatic bath tub emanated from room No. 108 of the Capitol, rattled the doors and transoms. . . . It was the governor's wind up snore. Having completed his toilet he proceeded, surrounded by a body guard of faithful followers, where he fed himself with his knife with great eclat."

James Stephen Hogg was a politician who obviously inspired some and disgusted others. Impartial evaluations of his career are hard to come by, even more than three quarters of a century after his death. For example, the *Galveston News* said of Hogg in 1892:

> So much for the czar and the autocrat of Texas, this completest and most perfect specimen of the demagogue that the nineteenth century and all of the other centuries have produced. We are progressing in all other lines, but we expect and look for no further development of the line and deportment of political demagoguery. We have absolutely reached the climax in the finished, well-rounded, and symmetrically formed James Stephen Hogg of Tyler, Texas. Nature has done her part, has reached her highest point, has exhausted all her resources, and can do no more.

But when Hogg died in 1906, the same newspaper paid tribute to him as "the portly, good-natured, heroic ex-Governor" and allowed that "few men of this age have accomplished more than James Stephen Hogg." And until Ima Hogg's death in 1975, any historian or journalist who took on James Stephen Hogg also had to contend with his daughter, who, as it turned out, had not pasted all those clippings for nothing.

In 1946, *Life* magazine, in an article called "Booming Houston," identified Ima as "Houston's social leader . . . daughter of the late, extremely capable Governor James Hogg, whose bluff sense of humor apparently led him to choose Ima's name." This drew no response from the governor's daughter, but it provoked a close friend of hers, Faith Bybee, to write a letter to *Life*'s editor, Henry Luce, explaining how Ima Hogg had been named for the heroine of a Civil War poem. The Bybee letter was then quoted by Houston newspaper columnist

Ima Hogg

Ed Kilman in his *Houston Post* column, "Texas Heartbeats." In a piece entitled "How Miss Ima Was Named," Kilman recounted the story of how Ima Hogg had been named for the Ima in *The Fate of Marvin,* and allowed as how it might be true. But Kilman also told the story of how Ima and another little girl used to sit on the governor's campaign platforms "at more than one of his speakings. And on each occasion the big East Texan jokingly introduced them as 'my daughters, Ima and Ura Hogg.' "

That column, which appeared in the *Post* on November 10, 1946, did provoke a response from Ima Hogg. She wrote an indignant letter to Kilman, who ran it in his November 17 column. Said the governor's daughter: "I did accompany my father occasionally on some of his campaigns, but he permitted me to stay in the background, as I was quite a shy little girl and he respected my feelings. He had as delicate understanding of others as anyone I have ever known and would never have exposed his daughter publicly to the embarrassment of the introduction you quoted."

All her life, Ima Hogg worked at presenting her father's best side to the public. Articles like the one in the January 19, 1969, *Tempo,* the *Houston Post* Sunday magazine, were certain to bring down the wrath of Governor Hogg's daughter upon his detractor.

The day was unusually warm for January, even in Texas. Mounting the platform, the big man (he weighed close to 300 pounds) shucked his coat as he prepared to speak. Spying the pitcher of water, he poured a glass and gulped it down. It didn't make a dent in his thirst, so he lifted the pitcher with both hands and drank long and deep while the crowd watched, fascinated. The thirsty giant was James Stephen Hogg, the year was 1893, and the occasion was his inauguration for a second term as governor of Texas. In the throng that stood on the Capitol grounds to watch Gov. Hogg take the oath of office was an 11-year-old Austin lad, Max Bickler. It was his first inauguration, and he never forgot Gov. Hogg, the pitcher of water and the big fireworks display that night.

When Ima Hogg read this, she fired off a letter to the *Post*'s "Sound-Off" page:

I am indignant over Mr. Bickler's account of the second inauguration of my father, James S. Hogg. I was also present at the inauguration described by Mr. Bickler and I am about the same

38

age — 87. My memory is vivid about every detail of the affair, and I am sure Mr. Bickler is either confused or . . . made a curious attempt at humor. He knows there are few left to refute his statements. . . . Mr. Bickler meant either to be facetious or to ridicule my father when he said he drank out of a pitcher at the inaugural ceremonies.

Governor Hogg may or may not have drunk from the pitcher on the inaugural platform that hot day, but he had certainly done so more than once on the campaign trail. As C. V. Terrell, former state senator and longtime Hogg supporter, recalled:

> On one occasion, at Temple, he perspired freely and drank a great deal of water out of a pewter dipper. It took too much of his time and bothered him, so he threw the dipper on the table, picked up the cedar bucket with both hands, and drank from the bucket to the approval and delight of the crowds. After that he was always provided with a bucket of water but no glass or dipper. It was part of the show to see him drink from the bucket.

On the question of the water pitcher, Ima Hogg's memory and honesty almost overpowered her desire to protect her father's image, and she did admit in her letter that "actually, if the occasion at a campaign rally demanded it, he was equal to drinking out of a pitcher if no glass was available." That small quarter given, she disposed of her enemy with a parting shot: "I wish I had space to describe the glamour of the Inaugural Ball to which Mr. Bickler was not invited."

Ima Hogg not only remembered the 1893 inauguration, she no doubt remembered another ceremony in 1894, when she had gone on a tour to the East with her father, and he had been honored at a Liederkranz Society festival in Madison Square Garden. On that occasion Hogg had appeared onstage with New York's governor, Roswell Flower, and the two were offered some champagne. Flower accepted his, but Hogg, ever mindful of his audience, remembered he was at a German festival and asked for some beer. A huge schooner was brought out, and as Hogg lifted it, the crowd began to cheer, and they kept cheering as he drained the schooner of beer without a pause, just as the crowds in Texas had cheered when he drank from a water bucket. Amid the tumult, he said to Governor Flower: "By Gatlins, Governor, this is no wine crowd, and a man in politics must remember the people he happens to be with."

In 1928 historian Herbert Gambrell, in an article entitled "James

Stephen Hogg: Statesman or Demagogue?" offered a balanced account of Hogg's career as a crowd-pleasing politician and a reform-minded public official, and concluded that "Hogg was not at heart a demagogue although he practiced with unrivalled skill the arts of mob-psychology. He never advocated a program in which he had a selfish interest, nor did he profit financially by public office. And if he missed being a statesman, it was the fault of his lack of training — and it was by a narrow margin that he missed it — if at all."

Some years after this article was published, Gambrell wrote to Ima Hogg asking what she thought of the piece. He received the following reply:

My dear Mr. Gambrell:

After reading your article, "James Stephen Hogg: Demagogue or Statesman," I hardly know what comment to make; there is so much. You were kind to ask it, and a bit naive! I appreciate the opportunity.

My conclusion is that you are in doubt on both points of your subject. On your estimate of him as a statesman, I do not need to comment: his record is secure and the results not uncertain. There has been so little serious writing on my father in retrospect, it rather dismays me to meet a careful attempt like yours done with lack of understanding. Of course, I do not know what records have influenced you or what manner of friends or enemies. When I recall that among his intimates were such men as Chilton, Sawnie Robertson, LeRoy Denman, Thos. Franklin, Reagan, A. W. Terrell, Culbertson, Tom Campbell, T. J. Brown, Gossett, House, etc., etc., I feel proud of his discrimination. Colonel House volunteered the remark to me only a few years ago that in his contact and experience with men, he had not known my father's equal in ability or character. As a child I became acquainted too with many of his political enemies.

To understand and explain a character or personality like my father's, one needs more than the written word of that time. During his political career, the reports were so confused by bitterness and misstatement of fact, there is now danger of utter misrepresentation from these sources. I pasted all the scrap books during that period and am familiar with the unreliability of the press. There were fabulous stories too passed around about him even in his day, so it seems to me how can one expect to get light on him except from those intimate associates, some of whom could have been trusted to be impartial. Alas! now so

40

few remain. There is always so much to know about a person.

The undoubted picturesqueness of my father's personality was such a small, if potent and delicious, part of him. But he was no boor or slouch. His keen sense of humor and ever ready wit gave him equilibrium from an otherwise too earnest and sensitive disposition. Few men are so endowed with talent for leadership and living. Sometimes I think the spell which such men cast springs from a deep and sure love for humanity — *with* detachment. At least it was so with my father. His delight in nature, the reciprocal love of children, of birds and beasts were important things to him and he knew so much quite naturally about everything in their world.

My association was with him on his campaigns, in travel and in the home — a most unusual opportunity to know him and yet now in perspective my wonder has grown. Whence came his power, his unerring sense of justice and honor — his freedom and beauty of spirit — his whole philosophy so fundamental? I can only surmise from small, intimate incident and talk and from some knowledge of early influences and background.

Though simple and unpretentious in his life, his nature was as deep as his mind was clear. He enjoyed the uses and exercise of his mind. He regarded himself as a thinker so all of his habits were regulated to that end. While he professed no scholarship, he had well defined and unique ideas of purposeful reading and learning for himself. I have never known a more assiduous student or one with greater powers of concentration.

But I fear I could easily appear tiresome. Why can't you come down some weekend for a little visit — say from November 29th to December 2nd; anywhere along there. Bayou Bend, the home here, would make you a welcome guest as should I. You see, while I do not agree with your views, I found your article interesting.

Yours very truly,
Miss Ima Hogg

Although Ima Hogg was unable to make a convert of historian Gambrell, who never revised his article about Governor Hogg, a few years later she found a scholar who was willing to write a full biography of her father to rescue him from the charges of demagoguery laid upon him by at least three other historians: C. Vann Woodward, James Tinsley, and Reinhard Luthin. Robert C. Cotner was given full access to the Hogg papers in the University of Texas archives and shown around the governor's old stomping grounds in East Texas by Ima Hogg herself. *James Stephen Hogg*, his 586-page biography of Hogg, published in 1959, is a paean to the governor from start to finish. The preface gives some idea of the tone of the book: "Each year thousands of visitors to the rotunda of the Capitol of the State of Texas observe the portraits of the governors which cover the circular walls beneath the great dome. Many linger to ponder the expression of a full, jovial countenance which shows strength, determination, and kindliness, and whose blue eyes reflect candor — they are looking at the likeness of James Stephen Hogg, the man who, because of his interest in the plain people, is known as 'The People's Governor.' " Perhaps the best and fairest estimate of Hogg is University of Texas historian Joe B. Frantz's assessment of the governor in his 1976 history of Texas: "Earthy but not profane, this native son knew his people, how to criticize them, and how to move them. . . . Hogg was indeed the last people's governor of Texas, perhaps the only one."

Hogg's last term as governor was even busier than his first one, but Sallie's health was failing, and he devoted as much time as he could to his family. In the summer of 1894 Governor Hogg wrote to his wife from Oakland Beach, Rhode Island: "Ima is in the other room playing 'snap' with two little girls and a bachelor, while Governor Brown of this State looks on." The fond father ended his letter with "Well I must quit, as Ima is playing the *Washington Post March*, and the crowd demand my attention." The next summer, when Ima and her mother were in Colorado, Hogg kept constantly in touch with them by mail. In New York on business in June 1895, he wrote to Ima on his return to Texas:

My Dear Daughter:
Your sweet little letter of the 2d has reached me from New York to which place it was directed. I left there on the first day of June and nearly suffocated during the four days of travel in getting home. The weather is scorching hot here and I am rather miserable over it. The little brownies you sent me by former letter were cute and interesting and I missed the lioness your last one mentioned. Now it is too bad for you to be spending your time in writing and drawing with only bad pencils and inferior paper. Tell your Mother that I shall accept it as a great favor if she will get some nice material, for you certainly deserve it. From all I can learn you and your Mama will fatten up so we will hardly know either of you. Won't that be nice? No news.

The Governor's Daughter

Love to all. Kiss all the family for me. Goodbye,

Your Papa

After he left office, Hogg spent some time in the Northeast trying to attract investment capital to Texas, and Ima, traveling with her father, was included in virtually all his activities: "It was a very amazing and enlightening experience and Father seemed to believe that anything in which he took part was becoming for me also. The men on these trips were not restrained by my presence and used to sit around playing poker until late at night. Father gave me a chair around the table where we both looked on. They imbibed very freely of alcohol." But according to Ima, her father neither played cards nor drank on these occasions. He was, in fact, "a stickler for no alcohol except at home," where he "thoroughly approved of a toddy at home and wine at the table." It was on her travels with her father that Ima had her first glimpse of New York. She wrote later that the city was not as grand as Austin: "New York was a great disappointment to me! Broadway was not as wide as Congress Avenue. Macy's was not as stylish as Hatzfeld's; but the Fifth Avenue Hotel and Delmonico's were glorious enough." Glorious, indeed, for a twelve-year-old who had never been out of Texas. Her brothers Mike and Tom were still too young for such travels, but one cannot help wondering why Jim Hogg so often took Ima with him and not Will, who was then in his late teens.

It was Ima, not her brothers, who went with Jim Hogg in 1898 to see the United States flag raised over the Hawaiian Islands. Ima was then sixteen. (In her eighties, she once startled some Hawaiian visitors to Houston by remarking casually, "Ah, yes, I have met your queen.") On the return trip, Hogg had booked passage on a steamer that sailed up the West Coast to Seattle, because he had never seen that part of the country. But when they went aboard to select their staterooms, Ima began to sob, saying that she had an "awful feeling" and begging her father not to sail on that ship. Said her indulgent father, "Well, Sissy, I always believe in following a hunch. If you say we won't go on this boat, we won't go on it." They then booked passage on a boat to California, and when they arrived they learned that the boat bound for Seattle had never made port. It had been lost at sea with all aboard.

By the turn of the century the Hogg family no longer spent much time together in Austin. Mike and Tom were in school at the Carlisle Military Academy in Hillsboro; Will had started his own law practice in San Antonio; Ima had gone to New York to study piano; and Jim

43

Ima Hogg

Hogg, who had had to borrow money to move out of the Governor's Mansion in Austin, had begun to speculate in oil lands. He had done well in legal practice in a partnership with an old friend, James H. Robertson. The firm of Hogg and Robertson took in about $30,000 the first year — in the days when a dollar was a fair day's wages. Meanwhile, on January 10, 1901, the first gusher, Spindletop, had just come in on the coastal oil fields near Beaumont, and soon it seemed that all Texas was abuzz with schemes for getting rich. In March Jim Hogg decided to buy 4,100 acres of land on the site of the old Varner plantation near West Columbia. At the same time, he and an old friend, James Swayne of Fort Worth, formed the Hogg-Swayne Syndicate and obtained the mineral rights to 15 acres of land on the Spindletop mound, where they would have five wells by the spring of 1902. In the boom that followed the discovery of oil in the area, however, the price of crude oil fell to 3 cents a barrel. But hopes continued to run high, and Hogg believed there was oil on his Varner plantation property.

In January 1902 he wrote to Ima, who was still studying in New York: "The oil prospects are good. It may yet turn out to be a *gusher* of oil. As it is we have three veins of flowing oil, in paying quantities. . . . But we want a gusher, and we intend to have it — *if* we can *get it*; and we believe we can." A few weeks after this letter was written, the Hogg-Swayne Syndicate joined with J. S. Cullinan, Walter B. Sharp, and others to form the Texas Company, which would become better known after 1906 as Texaco. In those early years of the oil business, capital for long-term development was hard to come by, and Hogg could not interest the Texas Company in drilling at Varner. Despite his efforts, all that the Varner land produced during his lifetime was a herd of goats, some cattle, and some vegetables.

At the end of 1902 Will Hogg wrote a facetious letter to his sister: "Prepare to become a comfortably rich woman. Your land at Columbia has healthy prospects of proving gusher territory. Drilling near here, adjoining your estate, is progressing rapidly and James Stephen 'would not be surprised to see 'em gush by Christmas.' Don't begin to spend money on your prospects, just now. . . . I am your legal advisor and attorney."

Although the Texas Company grew steadily and paid substantial dividends (the corporation would be valued at $30 million by 1913), the Hoggs did not become independently wealthy from oil until 1919, when the West Columbia oil field came in. In the meantime Jim Hogg put his money into developing the Varner plantation as a model farm. By the fall of 1902 the old plantation had a thousand acres under cultivation, farmed by twenty-five black workers who produced English peas, strawberries, and other delicacies along with corn and potatoes. In livestock, Varner could boast 50 head of cattle, 16 mules, some flocks of geese, chickens, and turkeys, and 250 goats Hogg had bought to keep the grounds neat. In 1904 he added 2,000 heifers and 8 bulls to his holdings, and the *Houston Post* ran a story called "Jim Hogg, Agriculturalist."

Busy as he was with his law practice, oil speculations, political activities, and farming, Hogg was still a man who kept in touch with the people. A letter he wrote to a little boy who wrote to him in 1903, asking for a goat, is testimony to Hogg's homespun wit and warmth:

My Dear Little Friend:
Out of the thousands of calls on me for contributions, presents and assistance I find none so unique, terse and boy-like as yours; which simply asks me to send you a goat. I wish I had one here now to express to you, but I have none. Down on my plantation, several hundred miles from this place, I have some goats and I will describe them to you. There are big goats, and little goats, he goats, and she goats, white goats, black goats, red goats, blue goats, grey goats, yellow goats, speckled goats, long-horned goats, Angora goats, Spanish goats, fine goats, common goats, all kinds, classes and colors of goats, and each and every one of them is a book-eating, tree-skinning, briar-cleaning, snake-stamping, bucking goat, used for the purposes of clearing up the woods, brambles and thickets around the premises. Now, the first time you hear that I am in Houston, I want you and your brother to call on me at the Rice Hotel, so that you can explain to me whether or not one of these malicious goats which you call for would get your father into trouble with his neighbor. I warrant you are a nice boy, and I hope to make your acquaintance. With sincere regards, I am,

Your Friend,
J. S. Hogg

Since 1901 Hogg had had to do without the company of his daughter except at vacation times and summers at Varner. After two years at the University of Texas, eighteen-year-old Ima Hogg had gone off to study piano in New York. That was not quite as daring as it sounds, since she was duly looked after by a chaperone, a Mrs. Day, and was no doubt carefully sequestered in her studies at Mrs. Green's Conservatory on Fifth Avenue. At any rate, the family apron strings stayed firmly tied: Brother Will wrote to Ima, "Dear Sis, Please do not neglect your duty of writing them [Mike and Tom] a joint letter once a week. Don't forget to write me once in a while and your dear Daddy every day." Whether she actually did that or not, it is clear from her father's letters to her that the two had a special relationship. Hogg, on a business trip to London in 1902, wrote to his daughter: "I dined with Lord and Lady Deerhurst at their home and got a *glimpse* into English society. . . . How I missed you! In fact I miss you wherever I go. So you must excuse me for this boyish weakness, as I so much need you to keep me *straight!*"

Later that spring, after Hogg's return from England, Ima wrote to her father suggesting a trip to Europe for her younger brothers. She received the following reply:

> Now, Ima, that dream of yours won't work. I shall not indulge those boys in a "trip to England." I should not do so if I had the wealth of Carnegie. I never saw a "well travelled young man" that was worth kicking out of the back door! *My boys must work* their way! When they win their expense money they can travel with more pleasure and greater intelligence and benefit. Keep it before them that it is manly in them to succeed; that it is unmanly in them to spend the "Old Man's" money *except for an education and necessities while going to school*, if he should be fool enough to let them have it. Your influence over them will make fine men out of them. Of course I shall be glad to take you anywhere, if I have to make the boys work to defray the expenses. In other words, you shall have *carte blanche*, as you have always had and never abused.

Ima seems to have been the most dutiful of daughters, a fact that her father himself acknowledged: "You have so conducted yourself at all times; been so thoughtful of your brothers; so kind to me, and have devoted yourself so faithfully and successfully to your music that I am proud of you at all times." In 1900, when Ima was eighteen, she was beginning to go out in the company of young men—but she was conscientious about seeking her father's approval of her activities. On one occasion, after she had written to him of some excursion, he wrote back, "Dear Ima: That's all right! I know you and Miss Fanny Henderson must have enjoyed the gentlemanly company and the excellent entertainment." The rest of the letter is filled with fatherly advice about how a lady should conduct herself. Jim Hogg exhorted his daughter to remember that "a woman's character is her capital. When it is bad she is poor indeed."

Was Jim Hogg perhaps too possessive of his only daughter? In 1903 he wrote to her:

> I still keep my dress suit, like the one Will admired so at the Inaugural Ball, and am ready, willing and waiting — for *you!* Yes, for you to get out of school, and go out with me — at least once in a while; that is, at such times as it may be *convenient* to you, but thereon hang my "heavy hopes" — on a delicate thread: *When convenient* to you! I know my rivals to go with you will be much younger, more handsome, and — and — well, they cannot be more willing, nor at any time prouder of the honor.

In one of Ima Hogg's scrapbooks in the Bayou Bend archives is a faded dance program from the Texas State Medical Association Ball of 1904, with the name "Hogg" written in for three of the dances. One can be fairly certain that Jim Hogg did not drink out of any water pitchers on that occasion. In another of his letters (which he sometimes signed "Jym") he revealed an unconscious reluctance to hear about any rivals for his daughter's affections. While Mike and Tom and Ima were vacationing in New England one summer, Hogg wrote to Tom, "Tell me in confidence if you please if you have a sweetheart now and how you are getting along with her, and how about Mike's. . . . And do not tell about Ima's. She will do this herself."

There are indications that Ima, then in her early twenties, tried to maintain a degree of independence. In the summer of 1904 she hurt her knee, as an undated clipping in the family papers reports: "Miss Ima Hogg's Condition Serious." She had somehow thrust a needle into her kneecap and evidently suffered complications, but she tried to conceal the seriousness of it from her father. She was vacationing in New England, but a cousin, J. W. McDugald, wrote to Ima's father that he had heard that Ima was "again on crutches," and that it "was apparent . . . that Ima has been trying to conceal this matter for the evident purpose of avoiding giving you and her friends any uneasiness." Later Ima did mention the knee problem to her father, but casually: "By this time you know I am back in South Egremont on both legs." As if to reassure him, she went on to say she had been learning "tennis-playing." In another letter to her father in January 1905, written while she was in Austin with Tom, who had been ill, she wrote that "a good deal of entertaining is going on for Austin, so I shall be going some. Last night went to a dance, this afternoon to receive at a reception and to-night. Next week there will be a good many more receptions."

If any young men escorted her to the entertainments in Austin, or if any were among the visitors and weekend guests at the Varner plantation, they are not mentioned in the few family letters in the Hogg papers. If any suitors courted Ima in the big chairs on the veranda at Varner in those long-ago summers, their names are lost. She never reminisced about her girlish romances, and only a few scraps of evidence remain. In the archives at Bayou Bend, among the items preserved in a scrapbook are some faded handmade valentines, but these hopeful admirers did not sign their names. From the time she was thirteen, when her mother died, until she was twenty-three, Ima Hogg was a devoted companion to her father — the "sunshine of my household," he called her.

It was Ima who became her father's nurse and constant companion during what was to be the last year of his life. On January 26, 1905, James Stephen Hogg was injured in a train accident on the way from West Columbia to Houston. It was a minor collision with a string of boxcars, but several passengers, including Hogg, were thrown violently to the floor. His neck was injured in the fall; an abscess formed; a series of operations followed. Ima never left his side, often sleeping in the room with him, listening anxiously to his labored breathing. By April of that year he was sufficiently recovered to speak at a banquet in Dallas honoring President Theodore Roosevelt, but he never fully regained his strength. Hogg had once joked about heart trouble as the "fat man's fear," but now illness and surgery had taken their toll on a heart already strained by all the years of overweight.

The hot summer of 1905 was hard on him, even in the house at Varner, with its thick walls and high ceilings. In August he and Ima went to Manitou, Colorado, to escape the heat, but the altitude strained his weak heart even more, and in September he was worse than ever. Ima, worried, sent for Will to help them make the long train trip back to Houston. For a time that fall, her father grew better, and in November he was scheduled to speak at a meeting of state officials in Dallas. On the way there, however, he became ill in Fort Worth and was unable to continue his trip. To console him for not being able to address the Dallas meeting, at which four candidates for governor were to be present, the resourceful Ima arranged for him to make a recording of his speech from his hotel room bed in Fort Worth, and thus the politicians assembled in Dallas were able to hear Jim Hogg, after all.

When Hogg had recovered enough to leave Fort Worth, he was

taken to Austin, where he held forth in his suite at the Driskill Hotel. He stayed there until February, seeing old friends, writing letters, and following the doctors' orders not to return to his law office in Houston until sometime in the spring. Just that year he had decided to move to Houston and had formed a new partnership with Edgar Watkins and Frank C. Jones. Back at Varner, Hogg listened to his children's advice to have his condition evaluated by medical experts, and he planned to go later to Scott and White Clinic in Temple. Early in March 1906, he and Ima made a trip to Houston, where they stayed at the home of Frank Jones. On March 3, 1906, James Stephen Hogg died of a heart attack in his sleep.

His daughter was devastated. It was she who found her father dead in his bedroom at the Joneses' house. As the *Houston Post* reported it, "Miss Hogg's intense devotion to her father had often been remarked as a touching instance of filial constancy, and the sudden discovery that her father was no more prostrated Miss Hogg. She is now under care of a physician — a brave little woman with a bounteous heritage of fortitude from her father, which her friends declare will aid her in bearing her great bereavement." The *Houston Chronicle* also reported that "his daughter, stricken by the burden of her grief, is in the care of a physician."

Two weeks after Hogg's death, Ima's brother Will wrote to a family friend that she was "improving, but is still almost sick." Will was heartened, however, by Ima's resolve to go to New York and resume her music studies as soon as she was able. "She says that she can more quickly find herself in that way than she can by staying in Houston, Austin, or elsewhere." But more than four months later, she had not gone. Will wrote to their grandfather Stinson about her, worrying that "she has not been at all well since father's death" and that she was "still quite nervous and restless, especially of nights." By September of that year, however, Will took Ima and Tom, who was also suffering from poor health, to New York. Somewhat later, Will wrote again to his grandfather Stinson with some relief: "Sister has improved since going there and so has Tom." New York and music seemed to have worked their restorative powers, and in January 1907 Will wrote to a family friend, Colonel Edward M. House, that "Sister Ima came back very much improved, and in much livelier frame of mind, which, of course, is a great gratification to me."

Ima Hogg was obviously in a depressed state for a time after her father's death, and for the rest of her life she would suffer what appeared to be periods of depression — some more severe than others. Unresolved grief over the death of a parent, according to modern psychological theory, can cause depression. Ima Hogg had lost both parents before she reached her mid-twenties — and she had nursed each one through a prolonged and painful period of ill health beforehand, certainly cause enough for a depressed state of mind. In Ima Hogg's youth, however, mental illness of any sort, like tuberculosis, was little understood and often concealed. That may be one reason that Ima Hogg told Jane Zivley, her secretary and later the guardian of her personal papers, that she did not want anyone ever to write her biography. It may also have been the reason she never married.

That Ima Hogg triumphed over illness, whatever its nature (and, along the way, established the Hogg Foundation for Mental Health), is a tribute to her strength of character and will power. At ninety, looking back on her accomplishments, she mused in an interview for the Houston Metropolitan Research Center's oral history collection: "Everything I ever did, I had to struggle to do. . . . . It's odd. I never could do anything easily. I had to wait, and work, and try — until I finally did it." Only Ima Hogg knew what really lay behind those casual remarks.

After Jim Hogg's death Ima and her brothers had seen to it that his wishes concerning his grave were carried out: the night before he died, he had said that after his death he did not want any kind of stone memorial; he wanted a pecan tree and a walnut tree planted on his grave instead, so that the "plain people" of Texas could have the nuts to plant on their land. A stone monument was later erected in the Hogg family plot in Austin, but not long after his death the trees were planted according to Hogg's specifications. In 1926 the first crop of nuts from the trees weighed five pounds. They were duly distributed by Texas A&M University. In subsequent years the crop grew larger, but by the 1960s the old trees were dying, so on Arbor Day, 1969, Ima Hogg helped to plant a young Choctaw pecan and a Thomas black walnut at opposite corners of the Hogg family plot in Oakwood Cemetery in Austin.

In later years the family — especially Ima — saw to it that Jim Hogg's memory was preserved in other ways. In the Hogg family papers, the letters of condolence after Jim Hogg's death are carefully preserved. Among them is one from William Jennings Bryan: "I was proud to count your father among my close political and personal friends. Drawn to him years ago by his devotion to popular government, by his brave defense of popular rights and by his steadfast championship of the interests of the masses I have relied on him ever since as a supporter of every worthy cause. We shall miss his voice in our party's councils and the pleasure of my visits to your state will be lessened by his absence." A few years after James Stephen Hogg's death the State of Texas honored his memory by naming a new county for him: Jim Hogg County in South Texas was created in 1913, and in 1941 Jim Hogg State Park, near Rusk in Cherokee County, was opened. In 1931, when Texan John Nance Garner became Speaker of the U.S. House of Representatives, he was given a gavel made from a post oak rail split by James Stephen Hogg. The handle was made of pecan wood from a tree Hogg had planted when he lived in Mineola. (The gavel's new owner probably didn't care: thirty years earlier, in the Texas Legislature, he had been an anti-Hogg man.)

So that the people of Texas might not forget Governor Hogg, his daughter later collected his speeches and state papers, and had five 10-volume sets privately printed. She gave one set to the Rice University library, one to the Texas State Library in Austin, one to Southern Methodist University, and two to the University of Texas. In the 1950s, more than a decade before Bayou Bend, the Hoggs' River Oaks home, was opened to the public, Ima Hogg created a museum in memory of her father. She restored the family home at West Columbia and gave it to the State of Texas for a state park. The restored antebellum house contains some of the Hogg family furniture—a black horsehair parlor set, an ornate upright piano that Ima played when she was ten, and Governor Hogg's memorabilia.

Varner-Hogg Plantation State Park was formally dedicated as Texas' fifty-sixth state park on March 24, 1958, the 107th anniversary of Jim Hogg's birth. To mark the occasion Ima Hogg had commissioned and privately printed a pamphlet with a biographical sketch of her father. She later reconstructed James Stephen Hogg's birthplace at Rusk (the house had burned in 1937), and in Quitman, where her parents had lived after their marriage in 1874, she restored and furnished their first home, now open to visitors as the Honeymoon Cottage. Filled with Victoriana, the little frame bungalow is, according to one old friend of Ima Hogg's, an idealization of Jim Hogg's early life: "Sallie and Jim never had a piano, much less a spinet—but she put one there, anyway."

Today, when visitors go through Bayou Bend in Houston, one of the first rooms they see is Philadelphia Hall, exquisitely furnished by Ima Hogg with priceless eighteenth-century American pieces. Every object in the hallway, as in the entire collection, was chosen and arranged with the greatest of care. There is just one anachronism. On the wall opposite the staircase is a large oil portrait of James Stephen Hogg. To Ima Hogg, the governor's daughter, it always seemed perfectly fitting and proper.

51

4

Family Fortunes

For a time after her father's death, Ima Hogg, then in her twenties, seems to have gloried in a newfound independence. She lived for a time in an apartment at 1602 Travis in Houston, and in 1907 she sailed for Europe — and stayed for two years. An undated newspaper clipping in the Hogg papers describes her departure from Galveston aboard the German steamship *Hanover*, bound for Bremen. While "a band played popular songs and American and German airs," a tugboat decked in bunting and signal flags appeared alongside the ship and dipped its colors to honor Ima Hogg, its namesake. The Galveston firm of Sunderman & Dolson had named one of its "best steam tugs" after the governor's daughter. "The matter was a complete surprise for Miss Hogg," the newspaper said, "and she acknowledged the compliment in a most charming manner." She could hardly have done otherwise, but one wonders how she felt at having her name paraded before a shipload of passengers, some of whom must certainly have laughed. Perhaps she was relieved to disembark at Bremen, and to be in a place where German was spoken and the words "Ima Hogg" did not provoke immediate amusement.

She began to study music with Franz Xaver Scharwenka, who was pianist to the court of Francis Joseph I of Austria, and later she continued her training with another musician, Martin Krause, in Berlin. In the off-hours from her piano studies she savored the charms of pre–World War I Europe. More than six decades later, Ima Hogg would reminisce about those years with Wanda Toscanini Horowitz, who, as the daughter of the famous conductor, had grown up in Europe. When pianist Vladimir Horowitz and his wife visited Houston for one of his then-infrequent concerts, Wanda and Ima remembered how, in those happier days in Berlin, Kaiser Wilhelm used to ride his horse through the park.

As a rule, however, Ima Hogg never talked much about the time she

53

spent in Germany. It is tempting to speculate on what life there would have been like for a young girl in her mid-twenties, one who was an accomplished horsewoman, a graceful dancer, a determined and talented musician. Language would have been no problem, since she had had a Bavarian nursemaid and had studied German in school. One of the few clues to this part of Ima Hogg's life came to light some years after her death, when, in the attic storage area of Bayou Bend, some old photographs were found. One of them, which has since been lost, was a picture of Ima Hogg and a handsome young man. The two were smiling and were obviously more than casual acquaintances. On the back of the photo, in Ima Hogg's small neat handwriting, was written "Fritz and me." Was there a blighted romance? A promise to return? Perhaps a long-distance love affair snuffed out by World War I? Ima Hogg never spoke of any romantic attachments in those years, and the only evidence is her lifelong fondness for visiting Germany on her frequent jaunts to Europe — and perhaps her mysterious illness at the end of World War I, when she was hospitalized for nearly a year and convalescent for three more. Whatever it was, Ima Hogg was perhaps braver than anyone knew.

She worked intensely at her music during those years abroad, developing her technique and preparing for a career as a concert pianist. She came home, as her friend Nettie Jones recalled, "with a bone-crushing grip." But somewhere between Berlin and Vienna and Houston she decided that a concert career was not for her. Her reasons for doing so are to this day unclear, perhaps because she did not want them known. When she was ninety-two, in an interview for the Houston Metropolitan Research Center's collection of oral history, she seemed deliberately vague about her musical career: "I played all my life. I played when I was three years old, and I studied in Europe, with very great teachers, and they all encouraged me to be a professional concert pianist. I never wanted to do that. I said, 'No, I'm studying for my own pleasure.' I didn't want to do it. And I played until I was very ill and I was in bed so long. When I got up I was so weak. I couldn't play, and gradually I just had to give it up. . . . I don't have time now." But to a close friend some years before this interview, she once confided, "The great sorrow of my life is that I was never a concert pianist."

At twenty-seven, Ima Hogg had apparently forsworn both romance and a career, and she came back to Houston in 1909 to spend the rest of her life as the unmarried sister of the Hogg brothers. She would teach music, she thought, and train others for careers on the concert stage. For nearly a decade, until 1918, she taught piano to a small,

54

select group of students, some of whom went on to illustrious careers of their own. Her first two pupils, in fact, were Bessie Griffiths, who was to be a talented piano teacher in Houston for many years, and Jacques Abram, who went on to a career as a concert pianist.

While Ima seems to have had no romantic interests on her return to Houston (Mary Fuller, one of her closest friends at that time, recalled that "Ima was not interested in men"), she led an active social life, attending the opera in Fort Worth, going to the theater and the movie houses in Houston, giving dinner parties, entertaining friends such as Dot Thornton and Vivian Caswell, whom she had known since their University of Texas days. Her brother Will's diary entries during this period record bits of her schedule: "Miss Ima gives book party." "Lynch D takes Miss Ima & me in his car to Ball & Banquet of King — all over 3:15." ("Lynch D" was Lynch Davidson, a Houston businessman; the occasion was the NO-TSU-OH Carnival ball, an annual affair in early twentieth-century Houston.)

While Ima Hogg may have occasionally danced until the small hours, she also gave some time to matters intellectual and cultural. On February 23, 1913, for example, she and Will went to hear the famous author and social critic Jacob Riis (*How the Other Half Lives*) lecture on "The Making of an American" at the City Auditorium. But Houston was not Berlin nor Vienna, and it had only the thinnest of cultural veneers over its rough-hewn frontier origins. The City Auditorium, completed in 1910 at a cost of $235,000 (on the site of the present Jones Hall at Louisiana and Capitol), could, according to a contemporary description, "seat comfortably, 7000 persons, and the stage is one of the largest in the country." But there were only traveling attractions to play on that stage. Houston had no professional theater, opera, ballet, or symphony in those days. Saloons and horse barns still dotted the downtown area, and many miles of streets were yet unpaved.

The Houston Lyceum and Carnegie Library, with a collection of fourteen thousand volumes, had been open since 1904, and three miles from downtown on Main Street, the new Rice Institute of Technical Learning had opened its doors in 1912. Since 1884 part of Main Street had been lit by electric lights, and by 1911 there were seven movie houses, four theaters, and more than twenty skyscrapers, including the new *Houston Chronicle* building at Texas and Travis, and the sixteen-story Carter Building at Main and Rusk. The city, with a population that had doubled in the past ten years, from 50,000 in 1900 to nearly 100,000 by 1910, also had 117 churches, 6 dance halls, 36 pool halls, and 311 saloons. By 1912 there were thirteen thousand telephones in Houston, with long-distance connections to cities as far away as Chicago and St. Louis, if not yet to New York or Los Angeles. One could dine at elegant establishments like the Richelieu Cafe at 1010 Congress Avenue, which was "for ladies and gentlemen only," or perhaps at G. F. Sauter's Delicatessen on the corner of Travis and Preston, which boasted a "ladies' dining parlor" as well as a "gentlemen's restaurant and bar." But there were no museums, no magnificent parks and boulevards, no salons, and Ima Hogg missed the rich and varied cultural life she had known in Europe. Houston, with its traveling theatrical companies playing their one-night stands, and its vaudeville shows and occasional concerts, must have seemed a wasteland indeed. One of the grandest attractions Houston had to offer was the five-story Rice Hotel (a new eighteen-story one would be built in 1917), advertised as having "225 Elegantly Furnished Rooms, with & without bath," and a "handsomely equipped billiard hall" and "Vapor, Massage and Turkish Baths." For some years, Will Hogg kept his lodgings there.

In 1909 the Hoggs considered building a house on the corner of Jackson and Walker streets, and Will wrote to Houston architect Charles Jones that Ima had already planned the structure. But for some reason the plans were never carried out, and in 1910 Ima and Will moved into the Warrington Apartments at 1502 Fannin. A year later they moved to the Oxford, a block away at 1402 Fannin, where they lived for five years, and where they were joined by Mike Hogg in 1915. In 1918, however, Mike, Will, and Ima moved into a house at 4410 Rossmoyne, where they would live until the building of the house at 2940 Lazy Lane in River Oaks in 1927. (Tom, the youngest brother, was married and living in West Columbia at the Varner plantation by 1913, and not long afterward he and his wife, Marie, moved to Denver.)

While Will and Mike were occupied with their growing business ventures in oil and real estate, Ima taught her piano classes and thought about what she could do to bring some grace to a rough-and-tumble but vigorously growing city. By 1913 she was president of the Girls' Musical Society, a group organized in 1910. It had eighty-five members and three hundred associate members, and met at the members' homes on the second Tuesday of the month from November to June. (In the dog days of pre-air-conditioning summer in Houston, most cultural activities came to a halt.) Ima also served on the entertainment committee of a group called the College Women's Club, which organized a little theater group known as the Green Mask Players. Theater in Houston could get along with amateur productions and occasional touring shows, but Ima Hogg decided that this booming young metropolis ought to have its own symphony orchestra. New York had had its Philharmonic Society since 1842, the Philadelphia Orchestra had been founded in 1900, and she vowed that Houston should not lag behind.

And so in 1913 Ima Hogg laid a plan before her friend Julien Paul Blitz, a Belgian cellist then living in Houston. Active in the city's cultural affairs, he was musical director of the Treble Clef Club, a men's musical group that met every Monday at the First Congregational Church. Ima persuaded Blitz to enlist other musicians in the city for a trial concert. Houston at that time had few musicians of symphony orchestra caliber, and almost no suitable hall for them to perform in. But Ima Hogg was not to be discouraged. On June 21, 1913, the *Houston Post* announced, "First Concert of Houston Symphony Orchestra at Majestic Theater at 5 p.m." An orchestra of thirty-five musicians, conducted by Blitz, played a program that began with the Mozart Symphony in E flat and ended with a rousing rendition of "Dixie." It was sandwiched between the Majestic's matinee and evening vaudeville shows. For the audience, seldom had devotion to the fine arts demanded such fortitude: the Majestic Theatre had only open windows and wall fans for a cooling system, and the temperature on that June afternoon was in the nineties. The concert hall was, as the *Post* music critic noted, "intensely warm."

Encouraged by the success of this first concert, Ima Hogg and others set to work in earnest to organize an initial season for the orchestra. Said a friend years later, "I remember the early days when she trudged up and down Main Street getting ads for the symphony programs. . . . Ima had an enormous facility for getting people to work for her. It wasn't that she wasn't hard on you, but she was equally hard on herself."

Ima Hogg worked doggedly to make a symphony orchestra a reality, but as always, she was modest about her efforts. When Hubert Roussel was writing his book about the history of the Houston Symphony in the early 1970s, Ima Hogg, looking over part of the manuscript, struck out the word "the" in a phrase describing her as the founder of the orchestra and changed it to "*a* founder." She saw to it that 138 guarantors pledged $25 each toward the Houston Symphony's first season: three concerts during the winter of 1913–14, to be conducted by Julien Paul Blitz. (Will Hogg, on December 19, 1913, wrote in his diary: "Houston Symphony Orchestra 1st concert 5 pm Majestic Theatre.") When the symphony's board of directors was formed, Ima Hogg modestly agreed to take the office of vice president, leaving the presidency for Mrs. Edwin B. Parker, one of Houston's cultural pillars and the wife of a prominent lawyer. But in 1917 the board of directors prevailed upon Ima to accept the presidency, and her involvement in symphony affairs, except for the brief period when she was ill in the early 1920s, never waned for the next half-century. She served twelve terms as president, founded the Women's Committee, engineered fundraising campaigns, and maneuvered, always delicately, to secure the best possible artistic and financial leadership.

In the years before World War I broke out, Ima Hogg continued to teach music. She kept up her own dexterity at the keyboard, and her knowledge of music was an added bonus in her work with the symphony. She also traveled a bit: in the summer of 1913, after the symphony drive was finished, she and Julia Ideson (who later became the city's librarian, and for whom the original library building at 500 McKinney is named) went off on a trip to the West Coast. In the spring of 1914 Ima went to New York with her brother Will, and Will's diary notes a round of theatergoing and dining out. The two saw Maude Adams in *The Legend of Leonora*, which Will thought was "fair."

Will was spending more and more time away from Houston on his various business interests, but his sister was quite able to fend for herself, as a letter from Ima to Will in April 1914 suggests: after thanking him for showing her such a good time on a recent visit to New York, she told him about a "gentleman burglar" who had surprised her before dawn one day in the ground-floor apartment on Fannin Street. "Also I had a gentleman burglar visit my boudoir yesterday morning. I didn't scream, and he put down my things after a nice calm little conversation. Mickie was awfully disappointed to think I handled him all alone. He would have loved to scold him or whipped him. White man, and said he'd made a mistake, thought Bill Anderson lived here. I took his word, but was careful to see he had nothing of mine. Awfully proud to think I didn't scream."

A few months later, this independent and self-possessed young woman sailed for Europe and arrived just in time for World War I. She had decided to make the trip on an impulse. Will's diary for June 10, 1914, observes that "Miss I proposes to go to Europe." The very next day, June 11, he wrote, "Miss I and I take Interurban at 1 pm for her to take 'Chemnitz' . . . for Bremen."

Two weeks later, on June 28, Archduke Francis Ferdinand of Austria and his wife were assassinated by a Serbian terrorist at Sarajevo, and by August the great powers of Europe were at war. Will Hogg, anxiously following the course of events, was no doubt relieved to hear from his sister on August 5: "Cable from & to Miss Ima who landed in London today (?)." She landed at a time when many tourists were turning homeward: England had declared war on Germany the preceding day. But Ima Hogg did not turn back. Apparently undaunted, she stayed until well into fall. She wrote home at least twice, as Will noted later in his diary, but she did not come back until October. When she did sail, space aboard ships was at such a premium that she had to share a stateroom with four-year-old Elizabeth McClendon, the daughter of the McClendon family of Austin. They took turns sleeping on the floor and in the one berth. Ima arrived home none the worse for her travels, however. She went riding with Will the day after her return to Houston, and two days later, she and Mike and Will went to the Majestic Theatre.

When the United States finally entered the war in 1917, Mike Hogg was commissioned as a lieutenant in the 360th Infantry, 90th Division, and was later promoted to captain. He was on active duty in the St. Mihiel and Argonne offensives and was wounded in the fall of 1918, just before the war ended. He came home in April 1919. Will met him in Norfolk, Virginia, and then the two went to New York to celebrate Mike's homecoming by shopping for his new civilian wardrobe at Brooks Brothers and seeing some shows. The brothers arrived in Houston on April 18 for what should have been a joyous homecoming. But all was not well with their sister.

Late in 1918, Ima Hogg fell ill. The exact nature of her illness will probably never be known. To judge from the scraps of evidence in the Hogg papers and the recollections of some persons who were close to her, it is likely that she suffered from some type of depression. She had been in a depressed state for a time after her father's death, but then she had been able to effect her own cure by immersing herself in her music studies in New York and later in Europe. This time, she was apparently very ill indeed. Her illness came on just after the armistice ended World War I in November. It is possible that this depression (if that is what it was) was brought on by the death of another person that she loved. In later years Ima Hogg never talked about her illness in specific terms, nor did she ever mention the young man with her in the photograph taken in Germany before the war. One cannot help wondering if somehow he and the mysterious illness are connected. Whatever the cause of Ima Hogg's depressed state in 1919, she eventually triumphed over it. She kept the battle secret, and probably no one will ever know how hard it was to win.

In January 1919 Will wrote to Marie, Tom's wife, that "Miss Ima shows improvement. . . . News of Mike's safety [after the battle of the Argonne, where he was wounded] has stimulated her and fresh news of Tom's recovery [from eye surgery] will stimulate her a great deal." But somehow she did not progress as Will had hoped, and his diary, with its brief, hastily scribbled entries, provides only the barest record of what must have been a time of anguish for the Hoggs. On April 21, 1919, Will and Mike arrived home from a business trip to New Orleans to find their sister's condition worse: Will wrote that day in his diary, "Find Miss Ima sick abed—Nurse & Dr. Taylor[.] Mrs. Thompson [the Hoggs' housekeeper] met us at 10:30 am train." Three days later he wrote, "Dr. Taylor and I discuss Miss Ima's condition." A diary entry for May 3, a few days later, noted hopefully, "Miss Ima dresses for dinner." But the next day Will wrote: "Miss Ima—Mrs. Lamb (nurse) & I start to Dr. Dercum at Phila." On May 7, the day they arrived, the diary entry reads: "Take Miss Ima to 'Rest House' at 1929 Wallace." That same day, Will went to see Dr. Francis X. Dercum, a noted neurologist and specialist in the treatment of nervous and mental diseases at Jefferson Medical College in Philadelphia and the author of several books, among them *A Clinical Manual of Mental Diseases* and *Rest, Suggestion, and Other Therapeutic Measures in Nervous and Mental Diseases*, both published in 1916. Ima Hogg was under Dr. Dercum's care for more than three years, including nearly a year in the "rest house" in Philadelphia.

In June 1919 her stay at the rest house was complicated by a mastoid condition that required surgery. Will's diary for September 7, 1919, indicates that she was on the way to recovery at last: "Miss Ima sitting up & doing fine." But on October 20 he wrote that he had received a "depressing letter of 15th from Dr. Dercum about Miss Ima's poor condition." Will spent Christmas of that year in Philadelphia to be near his sister, noting that she had a "private Xmas tree with her two nurses etc. Quite happy but not well by any means." Will visited Ima again in January, bringing with him a Pomeranian puppy named Buttons. He noted with some satisfaction that Buttons had the intended effect: "Missima & nurses—all delighted etc." Ima's recovery came later that spring. In March Will wrote to Tom that "the last news from Miss Ima is quite encouraging, and I now believe she is on an assured road to recovery. Dr. Dercum writes very optimistic and her own notes are very buoyant." Toward the end of the month she was apparently so much better that she was able to leave the rest house, and she continued her convalescence in Merion, Pennsylvania, a suburb of Philadelphia, until July. She spent the summer and part of the fall at a resort at Lake Placid, New York, where Will joined her from time to time. The Hoggs' oil field at West Columbia had begun to produce, and Will now had an apartment on West Forty-fourth Street in New York, where he spent an increasing amount of time.

Ima joined her brother in New York in October, and he did his best to lift her spirits, taking her to the theater and trying to interest her in her surroundings. On October 20, 1920, he wrote in his diary: "Miss Ima & Mrs. T [Mrs. Thompson, the Hoggs' housekeeper] & I look over some furniture around the town & they come by my apt after lunch at Claridge's." But Ima went back to Merion on October 25 and apparently remained there until the end of the year. Will's diary is uncharacteristically blank from December 14 to the end of the year 1920, the last entry being a hastily jotted note: "Tickets: Chi to Roch."

In January 1921 Will and his sister shopped and lunched in New York, but she was clearly not well yet. On January 4 Will wrote, "Miss Ima tired out"; on January 6, "Missima sick"; on January 15, "Miss Ima returns to Merion." By April, however, she was well enough to travel to Texas, where she visited at the home of her old friend Dot Thornton in Austin and attended the first annual meeting of Hogg Brothers, Inc., in Houston. This was the corporation created to manage the family's oil and real estate interests. It was owned entirely by Will, Ima, Mike, and Tom, all of whom attended its first annual meeting at Varner in April 1921. Ima, for a time, at least, was well enough to resume a normal life at the Hogg residence on Rossmoyne Street. A letter to her in May from her cousin Hermilla Hogg Kelso congratulated her on being "well enough to feel like taking the responsibility of the home." But in June, Ima was back in Philadelphia, and had another stroke of bad luck: appendicitis. On June 21 she had an appendectomy. Tom and Marie and Mike visited her, and Will, staying in New York, wrote in his diary on July 14 that she was "improving very much." By the end of the month she was well enough to go to Lake Placid and then to go to New York later in the summer to help Will decide on buying an apartment at 290 Park Avenue. In the fall of 1921 Ima was much better, and scattered entries in Will's diary record his joy at her recovery. September 2, 1921: "Miss I and I sup at Chatham Hotel & I loaf with her etc." December 13, 1921: "Stay at home [the new apartment on Park Avenue] & discuss matters with Miss Ima." Mike, Ima, and Will spent Christmas in New York, and in February 1922 they all returned to Houston. Will wrote happily on February 4, 1922, "Sunday in Houston. Loaf with MH & Miss Ima."

In April, Will Hogg, who had done as much as anyone to aid his sister's recovery, left for a month's vacation in Europe. The following year, in April 1923, Will, Mike, and Ima celebrated her improved condition by sailing for Europe. Ima had continued to see Dr. Dercum in

Philadelphia during the previous year, but by the summer of 1923 she was obviously fully recovered. Her brothers returned home in June; Ima did not come back from Europe until August. It was a well-deserved holiday. Ima Hogg had been ill off and on for nearly four years.

It was sometime during her stay in Philadelphia that Ima Hogg first thought about collecting antiques. Looking back on that time in her life years afterward, she recalled: "I used to walk for exercise down on Pine Street in Philadelphia. There was a little shop, and one man there that handled glass, and I bought little perfume bottles, and things that did not amount to much." In the little shop on Pine Street she met a "shabby-looking old man" who told her that she ought to collect glass. The man was William B. Montague, a wealthy carpet manufacturer and a major collector of Early American glass and ceramics. His collection of eighteenth-century slipware is now at the du Pont museum at Winterthur, and many years later Ima Hogg would buy some of his 1830s Tuckerware pieces for Bayou Bend.

The story of Ima Hogg as a collector might have ended here, with a few fine pieces of glass and ceramic ware acquired and later bequeathed to a museum, but Will Hogg, solicitous of his sister's health and anxious to speed her recovery, encouraged her interest in collecting antiques more than even she herself realized. In 1920 he had begun to collect furniture and art himself, buying antiques for the family home at Varner, which he was refurbishing, and acquiring art for his office in Houston. A diary entry for September 21, 1920, reads: "Buy 1 bronze *Bronco Buster* & 12 drawings & paintings of F Remington at Ainslie's Galleries." He would eventually have one of the finest Remington collections in the country. In 1921 he persuaded Ima to help him choose the furnishings for the new Park Avenue apartment, and it is possible that he and William Montague conspired to interest her in collecting — among the Hogg papers is an undated letter referring to a telephone call Will had made to Montague.

Whether or not Will arranged for Montague to meet his sister that time, there is no question that he encouraged her to pursue the study of American art and furniture. In 1921 he sent her a box of books: Mrs. Willoughby Hodgson's *Old English China* (London, 1913), *What Makes the House Beautiful*, edited by Henrietta Chandler Peabody (New York, 1920), *Modern American Sculpture*, edited by S. Hartmann (New York, 1918), and *Colonial Furniture in America*, by Luke Vincent Lockwood (New York, 1901). Sometime during this period Will arranged for Ima to have her portrait painted by Texas artist Wayman Adams, himself something of a collector of antiques. While

Family Fortunes

Ima was sitting for the portrait in his New York studio she noticed a simple maple chair. Made in the Queen Anne style sometime before the American Revolution, it had a curving back and a cane seat, and it was the first American-made antique she had ever seen. "I had no idea there was anything that fine made here then," she recalled later. She wanted to buy the chair from Adams, but he did not want to part with it. Will then went with her to one of the first New York dealers in American antiques, a firm known as Collings and Collings. This elderly couple (the second Collings was *Mrs.* Collings) found a chair almost exactly like the one she had seen, except that, ironically, hers turned out to be in better condition and of somewhat finer craftsmanship. A few decades later, Ima Hogg wrote, "Recently I had the good fortune to be able to buy the Adams chair from his heir. Now I look at it and I cannot imagine why I was so excited over that simple chair."

But in 1920, before she could buy the first chair from Collings and Collings, she had to convince her brother Will that the chair was worth the price. (One wonders if Will only pretended to be reluctant, knowing his sister liked nothing better than to talk people into things.) The chair, said Ima, "was so costly I couldn't get my brother excited about buying it. . . . I told him, 'We have a rare opportunity — to collect American antiques for a museum in Texas. It's never been done before.'" That first chair, now known as the Queen Anne maple Spanish foot chair, reposes in a place of honor at Bayou Bend, where docents recite its history to visitors in reverent tones. The Wayman Adams portrait of Ima Hogg hangs above it.

If Will Hogg had hoped to give his sister a consuming interest, he certainly succeeded. She was to spend the next fifty years hunting for Early American furniture and paintings, not to mention glass, ceramics, pewter, and silver.

As Ima Hogg entered the fortieth year of her life she had little enough to sustain her: her youth was gone; she had neither a marriage nor a career. For the next few years she led a quiet, almost reclusive life. The Roaring Twenties passed her by. She did not resume her activities with the symphony until 1927, and she spent long periods of time away from Houston, traveling in Europe and looking for antiques along the eastern seaboard of the United States. During these trips she did not keep in close touch with her brothers. A letter of Mike Hogg's in February 1926 notes that Ima was "somewhere in the East." In May of that same year Will wrote that she had gone to Europe: "She will return this summer, I think." In the fall of 1927 Tom Hogg wrote to his brothers from San Antonio, "Someone told me last night that Miss Ima was back and was looking fine. Was certainly glad to hear it." That same year Will wrote to a family friend that his sister was "getting too fat though she is in fine health and spirits." It is possible that during those years Ima Hogg's mental health required further treatment, and that she spent some time at an institution in the East. Architect John Staub, in an interview shortly before his death in 1980, said he had always suspected that she had been institutionalized briefly, "at Silver Spring, or someplace like that." In the meantime, her brothers Will and Mike were building a fortune in oil and cotton and real estate and leading the lives of men-about-town.

Although there was a strong bond of affection between the brothers and their sister (to amuse Ima, Will once had letterheads printed that read, "MISS HOGG AND BROTHERS, Cable Address MISSOG"), she was obviously not interested in their business and philanthropic activities. Ima Hogg's life during most of the Jazz Age seems to have been a quiet one. So much so, in fact, that when the *Houston Gargoyle*, a weekly magazine, featured a column of tongue-in-cheek New Year's resolutions for 1928, Miss Ima Hogg was quoted as resolving that "having become wearied with the gay round of Houston's night-life, I shall during 1928 go in for long and thoughtful sessions at Houston's Museum of Fine Arts."

Ima Hogg was a private person in her middle years, shy and retiring, but her eldest brother more than made up for her withdrawal from the public view. Will Hogg, large of girth, expansive of mind, gargantuan in appetite, and explosive in temper, was the driving energy behind Hogg Brothers, Inc., making his headquarters in a sumptuous penthouse atop the eight-story Hogg Building at 401 Louisiana in downtown Houston. There, surrounded by a roof garden lavishly abloom with shrubs and flowers, in a suite of elegantly furnished rooms that included an oval dining room, a kitchen, a living room, and a guest bedroom as well as offices, Will Hogg managed and enlarged the family financial interests in oil, cotton, and real estate, raised money for various philanthropic enterprises, and carried on his personal campaign for better civic and state government.

Will — who had graduated from the University of Texas law school in 1897 at the age of twenty-two, practiced law for a brief while in San Antonio, and spent some time in St. Louis before settling in Houston after his father's death in 1906 — had been a serious young man in his youth. He had deliberated long and hard about what kind of law he should practice and where he should practice it, and apparently his private life was conducted with equal solemnity. An 1899 letter to Will from Ellen Slayden, a family friend, advised him to enjoy himself more: "You need a dress suit, and you ought to dance, and you ought to be young instead of trying to begin at the end." As he grew older, Will Hogg would take that advice, more than making up for that lost youth. In his early years, however, he had reason enough to be serious.

After his father became ill, it was Will who had to manage the family's affairs, and when his father died it was Will who took on the responsibility of educating two younger brothers and providing for an unmarried sister. Mike and Tom had been sent to Lawrenceville School, a preparatory school in New Jersey, and while Mike would attend the University of Texas and the law school as Will had done, taking a law degree in 1911, Tom, the youngest of the Hogg children, was apparently a disappointment to the family. He did poorly at school in Lawrenceville, even with tutors, and a progress report in 1904, when he was seventeen, noted his "frequent indisposition." At age twenty he enlisted in the U.S. Navy, and his grandfather Stinson wrote to Will in the summer of 1907, "Sunday's Dallas *News* published his enlistment. . . . It was and is a pitiful situation. He may be headstrong self willed restless and indeferent [sic] . . . but there is a great *heart* in him."

Problems with his eyesight forced Tom to leave the Navy soon after he had entered it, and for a time he wandered about South America and Mexico before coming back to "make a great success as a hog farmer" (as an undated clipping in the family papers put it) on the Varner plantation in 1913. Tom was, for some reason, estranged from the rest of the family for a time, especially after the death of his father. He hired a separate attorney, for example, to protect his interest in the settlement of James Stephen Hogg's estate. Under the provisions of their father's will, Ima was to receive two thirds of the value of the Varner plantation property; Mike would have the remaining one third; and Tom and Will would share the mineral rights. A letter of Will's to his lawyers in 1910 refers to Tom's "frenzied and zealous hate for me," but by 1913, at least, a reconciliation had taken place. Tom and his new wife, Marie, often came in from West Columbia to visit Ima, Will, and Mike in Houston.

At that time Jim Hogg's children, though quite well off, were not rich by any means. Will would have liked to sell Varner, but a provision in the will forbade the family to sell any of the land at West Columbia for at least fifteen years after Jim Hogg's death. Six days after his father died, in March 1906, Will had written to the caretaker at Varner: "If you knew the condition of father's affairs you would readily appreciate our requests to keep expenses and advances to the negroes down to the minimum."

Ima Hogg

In 1919, however, oil was struck on the Varner land, and the West Columbia field made the Hoggs independently wealthy. By 1920 Will could write to his brother Tom in Denver that the average monthly gross income from the oil came to $225,000 — which meant that after some of the profits had been set aside for income taxes, there would be more than enough to "grub-stake" Ima, Mike, and Tom so that they could invest it and live on the income. Tom, who by this time had moved to Colorado and was working on the *Denver Post* in the advertising department, was advised by Will to go into investment banking, and in the summer of 1920 Will suggested that after a year or two in that business, Tom could join the Hogg Brothers, Inc., establishment in Houston. Tom, as usual, did not follow his brother's advice. Instead, he wrote that he expected to be in Houston in the fall for a visit, but "in the meantime I shall play around Colorado and Wyoming." By 1924 Tom and Marie had settled in San Antonio and were building a house, and Will was worried about the rate of Tom's spending.

In the spring of 1924 Will wrote to Marie that she must try to live within their means and see that Tom curtailed his extravagances — a warning that apparently had been issued before. Said Will: "I was forced to explain to you more than once the effort I have made to keep Tom within bounds so that you and he would not assume a scale of living that you could not maintain indefinitely. . . . Suppress your Rolls Royce vanities until we can accurately ascertain our real financial worth." In the Hogg family papers, scattered financial statements and itemized expenditures (ranging from horse feed to jewelry) from Tom are intermingled with letters from Will exhorting him to be more cautious with his money. In 1924, after Tom and Marie had spent $153,000 on building and furnishing their new home, Will Hogg's attorney, David Picton, wrote to Tom with the warning that "your withdrawals are so much heavier than that of the others." Family relations remained cordial, however, with Tom writing concerned letters about Ima's health and regaling his siblings with accounts of his efforts at breeding horses and raising dogs in San Antonio.

Some would say that Will and the others were extraordinarily patient with their youngest brother, who never seemed to learn either moderation or frugality. Will, writing to Marie Hogg in 1928, summed up his own attitude toward the family's fortunes: "The uppermost desire of my life is to have all members of the Hogg Family live decently and comfortably but not rampantly and 'nouveau-richly,' if you gather what I mean — live decently and wholesomely and contribute whole-heartedly and generously to the welfare of the community in which we live. Also, Mike, Miss Ima and I had hoped that

66

Tom would learn to live within his allowances and I will say he has improved somewhat during the last year or two."

Will Hogg took his own advice, although his idea of living "decently and comfortably" eventually included a Park Avenue apartment, a ranch in Mexico, frequent trips to Europe, and one of the finest collections of Frederic Remington paintings in the country. They hung in his rooms atop the Hogg Building, in his office; they complemented the Remington bronze, *The Bronco Buster*, that he had bought in 1920. The furnishings in the Hogg offices, one friend remarked, were "massive, but in good taste." There was "that big, hand made chair that had to be provided for him because he overflowed the regulation-sized seating facilities, as he overflowed everything else he touched." This same friend, Guy McLaughlin, once wrote to another of Will's friends, John A. Lomax, that "Bill Hogg was tough as a boot and tender as a woman." Will, who whimsically signed his letters to family and friends "Bilog" or sometimes "Blog," once told McLaughlin that the reason he had never married was that he was "not fit to marry." But McLaughlin speculated in a letter in 1939 that "the bond among Will C. Hogg, his sister Miss Ima Hogg, and Mike, his younger brother, was too strong to be broken by the marriage of any one of them." Mike would marry in 1929; Will and Ima, never.

For Will Hogg, however, this reluctance to marry did not mean the avoidance of female company. There were rumors of feminine guests and goings-on in the guest suite of the Hogg Building penthouse — and Will never actually denied them. He was nothing if not honest. On one occasion, recalled some years after Will's death by both John Lomax and Guy McLaughlin, Will Hogg had been quite frank about his relationship with a woman. The occasion was an appearance before a grand jury to supply information about one of Hogg's neighbors. Lomax told the story in a 1939 letter to Edward Weeks, the editor of *Atlantic Monthly*, when he was at work on a sketch of Will Hogg for that magazine:

"Mr. Hogg," said the foreman, "we are investigating a young woman who has a small cottage near your home. We understand that she is a widow living alone with one child. Our information is that she receives an unusually large number of gentleman callers, some at quite late hours. Can you throw any light on this situation?" Will Hogg rose and spoke somewhat as follows: "Mr. District Attorney and Gentlemen of the Grand Jury: . . . I find this group of thirteen of the leading citizens of Harris County devoting their time and taking my time in investigating the conduct of a poor defenseless widow, whose husband died two years ago, leaving her helpless and penniless. I don't know why she has gentleman callers, I don't know how often they drop in, and I don't give a damn. But what I want to ask you gentlemen is this: why don't you jump on somebody your size? Listen to me. I keep a woman at 204 Victor Street; Mr. J. C. Black keeps a woman at 908 Main Street; Mr. T. V. Jones keeps a woman at 2002 Carondelet; Mr. A. W. Rice keeps a woman at 308 Nueces." On he went until he had called the names of eight or ten of Houston's millionaires. "I'll go further," continued Will Hogg: "I'll sign a complaint against each one of these men, I'll agree to name witnesses that will prove my charges against them all, including myself. Now, by God, come on and go after us and leave that little widow woman alone. Good morning, gentlemen." And putting on his hat he walked from the room.

Lomax explained to Weeks that he could not print this anecdote on Ima's account, but, he said, "I wished to share this Will Hogg story with you anyhow. In it is epitomized the man whom I cannot even faintly begin to describe."

John Lomax had been close to Will Hogg since the controversial days of 1916, when Hogg did battle against Texas governor Jim Ferguson for firing six University of Texas faculty members (including Lomax) without good cause. Next to his family, one of Will Hogg's strongest attachments was his alma mater, the University of Texas. He served on the Board of Regents from 1913 to 1917, and when his term ended in the summer of 1917 he rented a suite at the Driskill Hotel in Austin and organized the campaign that led to Ferguson's impeachment, sending circulars about the firing of the faculty members to Texas alumni and buying advertisements in Texas newspapers charging that the governor had "put the putrid paw of politics" on the state university. For this and for misappropriation of state funds, Ferguson was impeached and found guilty. When the governor was removed from office (his successor was Lieutenant Governor William P. Hobby), Will Hogg rejoiced. His bitterness toward Ferguson placed him in an awkward spot later, when Ferguson ran for the U.S. Senate against Earle Mayfield, an avowed supporter of the Ku Klux Klan, and again when Ferguson's wife, Miriam, ran for the governorship against another Klan candidate, Judge Felix Robertson. Hogg, never in sympathy with the KKK, had to choose between supporting his political enemies or endorsing a candidate whose Klan backing he abhorred —

but in both cases he chose the Klan candidates rather than the Fergusons. Said Hogg of the 1924 governor's race: "It's a hell of a mess." That, for a man with Will Hogg's powers of expression, was an understatement, indeed.

Will Hogg inherited not only his father's girth (he generally weighed more than two hundred pounds) but his gift for picturesque language as well: said Will, engaged in a game of pitch at the Houston Club, to a well-dressed stranger looking on, "Come on in. You're as welcome as horse shit in a garden." Of Robert E. Vinson, an extremely religious University of Texas president whom he did not like, Will wrote, "He's a Fundamentalist from Fundamentalistville." Of the ranch in Mexico that he owned with a business associate, Raymond Dickson, a spread with thousands of cattle and a Spanish castle in the middle, Will said, "It's just a little patch with a sick cow and a sour well." Warring against Jim Ferguson, then in the U.S. Senate, Will printed a pamphlet entitled *57 Varieties of Fergusonism*. When Houston schoolchildren raised the money to purchase an equestrian statue of Sam Houston (the one now standing at the entrance to Hermann Park) and a committee debated whether or not Houston should be on horseback, Will Hogg put an end to the deliberations: "Hell, yes, let 'em put it up. It represents something; let 'em put it up. I don't give a damn if it's made out of horse manure and empty sardine cans, and the horse has a colt the next day—let 'em put it up."

On other occasions Will Hogg had been known to swear far more colorfully, and his reputation for picturesque profanity was exceeded, perhaps, only by that of his father. Edward Crane, who knew both father and son, once recalled seeing ex-governor Jim Hogg in action at a raucous party meeting in Waco in the summer of 1900. A hostile crowd was trying to shout Hogg down, but

> in a lull in the howling, like a pistol shot the words "You white-livered sons of bitches" broke clearly into the air. The gang was arrested in their demonstration. They wanted to hear the rest of it. Never will I expect to see a finer demonstration of sheer physical courage than that manifested by Governor Hogg. He cussed that bunch, individually and collectively, with every word in the English language. . . . The sheer courage of the man gripped that mob and before he had concluded, they were shouting his praises stronger than the demonstration against him.

If Will Hogg was a match for his father in vocabulary, he also had the temper to go with it. Once, returning in good spirits from a trip abroad, he appeared at his office, which had been newly redecorated and painted in his absence. He sent for his staff and announced, "I'm going to keep my temper, boys, and not fly off the handle any more. I realize it doesn't add anything to efficiency or your peace of mind." Then his office manager handed Will a stack of papers to sign. He picked up a pen on his desk, tried it on a piece of scratch paper, found it did not work, tried again, and then, as Guy McLaughlin described it, "he rose from his oversized chair, and with all his force threw the pen, slapdash across the room against the newly finished, artistic tinted wall." On another occasion Hester Scott, who worked for Hogg at the Houston Forum of Civics, wrote him a letter about his temper: "Because of your strongly dominant personality you do not get the best out of those who are associated with you. Your method of 'bawling them out' instead of getting the desired results, simply kills all initiative. . . . In the time I have been associated with you, I have never heard you listen to a single suggestion from anyone."

Will Hogg — big, blustery, dynamic, domineering (some people called him William "C. for Combustible" Hogg) — could be, when he felt like it, equally gentle and considerate. Once, on a train returning to Houston from San Antonio, he overheard the conductor talking to a woman passenger whose husband had just been found dead in his Pullman berth. The conductor was explaining that state law required the body to be put off the train at the next stop. Will Hogg took the conductor aside and told him he couldn't put a dead man and his widow off in "some jerkwater town." Telling the conductor he would take full responsibility, Hogg wired ahead to Houston and then spent the remainder of the trip sitting beside the grief-stricken woman, fetching her paper cups of water and trying to comfort her. When the train pulled into the Houston depot, Ima was there to meet it, waiting with her arms full of flowers. When the woman was last seen, Ima and Will each had an arm around her and were shepherding her toward their waiting limousine.

On another occasion, when Will was in New York, he and a party of friends had dinner at Dinty Moore's restaurant. When they were finished, he reached for the check, looked it over, and pronounced it to be $11 too high. He summoned the waiter, informed him in no uncertain terms of the error, paid the correct sum, and waited for his change to be brought to the table. The friends waited, too, fearing an outburst of the famous Hogg invective on the hapless waiter. Instead, Will reached into his pocket, took out some money, and said to the waiter, "Here, you good-for-nothing bastard!" Counting out the bills, he grinned and said, "On that deal I figure you make five and a half, and *I* make five and a half."

Usually a careful man where money was concerned, Will Hogg could, when he chose to, throw caution to the winds. Late one night in New York he was walking the streets by himself and spied a car in a showroom window. There was a light burning in a back room in the building, and Hogg, banging and calling out, finally managed to make his presence known. "I want to buy that car," he said to the bewildered car dealer.

"But it's after midnight," the dealer said. "I can't sell it to you now. I don't have any idea who you are, and I can't take a check at this hour. Come back in the morning."

Said Will, undaunted: "Who asked you to take a check?" He pulled out his wallet, counted out $5,000, handed the money to the dealer, and drove away in his new car.

Will Hogg could afford to be impulsive with his money. In the years after his father's death his financial affairs had prospered, and he was independently wealthy in his thirties. He and J. S. Cullinan and James L. Autry had formed the Farmers Oil Corporation; he was involved in the construction of a deep-water port on Corpus Christi Bay; he had a cotton warehouse; he dealt in real estate through the Varner Realty Company; he developed River Oaks, Houston's posh residential neighborhood.

Although he chose business and not politics as a career, Will Hogg inherited his father's sense of public duty, and he devoted much of his time to fundraising efforts for various causes and much of his fortune to a host of philanthropic schemes. The memory of James Stephen Hogg was a great influence on his son, as he told John Lomax. Recalling the time just before his father's death, he said:

Until that six months I spent talking with my father, I had never really known him. I had just taken him for granted. Then, for the first time, I understood why he had always espoused the cause of the common people, the need of battling for the weak against the strong, the necessity of free education for all, if a democracy is to survive. So I came to love more deeply this plantation, this farmhouse, and my father. Whatever little good I may do, whatever ideas may be found behind any action of mine, whatever has given my life any worth or dignity, all are due to him.

"The government," Will Hogg once said, "made a mistake originally

71

in not reserving for its own use all the wealth below the soil. What I don't pay back in taxes on the oil which should not have been mine, I'm glad to give away for the public welfare." For years Will Hogg told John Lomax, then secretary of the University of Texas Ex-Students' Association, "when any student in the University gets into trouble, help him. . . . If he needs money, lend it to him. If he is sick, get a doctor. If he gets thrown into jail, bail him out. If he dies and has no money or people, bury him. Don't wait to write or wire me; relieve the distress and then let me know what it cost. . . . And if you ever let anyone know where the money comes from, I'll never send you another blankety-blank cent."

When World War I ended (Mike had served; Will, forty-three and overweight, had not), Will Hogg authorized his alma mater to run advertisements in newspapers across the state announcing that any veteran who could qualify for admission to the university would be given a scholarship by an anonymous donor. Some five hundred applied, one hundred actually enrolled, and Will Hogg paid. To honor Houston's war dead, he planted magnolia trees along Shepherd Drive in the southwest part of the city. On the trees were nameplates bearing the names of Houston soldiers killed in World War I. Today, on the west side of the street, many of the memorial magnolias are still standing, but the nameplates have long since disappeared.

Many a student of the University of Texas had a scholarship paid for by Will Hogg, most of the time anonymously. He also gave money to at least fourteen other Texas colleges during his lifetime, and left money to several of them in his will. In addition, he provided money for several promising graduate students at UT to attend graduate schools outside the state. "In a well-ordered democracy," he once said, "no boy or girl with brains and character should be denied the opportunity of college training. I find that nothing else gives me half the satisfaction derived from the knowledge that I have gambled on the brains and ambition of young men and women. If I knew just when I was going to die, I wouldn't reserve enough money to buy a bowl of chili."

One of his first fundraising ventures was for a project to "stimulate thought and create and arouse, through bulletins and lectures, aspiration for higher education in Texas." Through the Hogg Organization, created in 1911, Will Hogg raised $25,000 in less than a year, and in 1912 a statewide Hogg Education Day gave prizes to more than a thousand students who had written essays on the financial and cultural values of education. The entire education project was to last five years and cost $250,000. Hogg traveled around Texas at his own expense raising the money. He vowed to spend his own resources if donors could not be found: "I'm worth a total of thirty thousand dollars. That's enough to run the shebang for a year. I'll dump that into the pot and let the doubters see the results."

Will also had long-range plans for the University of Texas itself. In 1913 he persuaded Texas governor Oscar B. Colquitt to introduce a constitutional amendment for a merger of UT and Texas A&M—a scheme that would have required, as Hogg saw it, the moving of Texas A&M to Austin. The existing facilities at College Station, he thought, could then be converted to an insane asylum or a reform school. But in the legislature the proposed amendment lost by one vote, 56–55.

The eldest son of Governor James Stephen Hogg, as large of frame and agile of mind as his father, could probably have been elected to any office he chose, but he declined to enter the political arena. He once wrote: "I'm not running for office and I never will. I won't wear a ball and chain on my leg while I am fighting those coyotes who are befouling the name of the State of Texas. I'd rather be a rock-throwing private soldier with a free voice than be the mouthpiece of an organization that would tell me when to talk and what to say." Not running for office did not keep Will Hogg from speaking his mind or taking action when he thought the situation demanded it. For example, when, on a trip to New York, he learned that the Board of Regents of the University of Texas had secretly sold a $3 million bond issue against university credit, he wired to cancel the transaction. The deed was done, but it took nearly a year to straighten out the accounts of the unknowing brokers who had bought in.

When he was not looking out for the interests of the University of Texas, Will Hogg was raising money for worthy causes. Brandishing a specially bound "blue book" with blank pages, he would persuade friends and business associates to sign their names and pledge financial support for projects as diverse as a home for disadvantaged boys, the YWCA, the Girl Scouts, and the Museum of Fine Arts. For these and other causes he waged what he called "a gumshoe campaign, highjacking my friends." Not only did Will Hogg raise money—over $300,000 for the Museum of Fine Arts (founded in 1922) and over $2 million for other organizations in the course of his life—he was equally munificent on his own. From 1914 to 1917 he was active in the Boy Scouts, serving as vice president and financial chairman of the local council. In 1919, while in New York, he was impressed by the new YWCA facilities he saw. He came home and began a campaign to raise $500,000 for a Houston YWCA, and the cornerstone of the new

73

building was laid in 1922.

To promote civic projects in gardening and landscaping, Will Hogg financed the printing and distribution of ten thousand copies of a color-illustrated *Garden Book*; to beautify the city of Houston, he bought thousands of flowering crape myrtle trees and gave them, free, to property owners. On each tree were two tags: one with instructions on how to plant and care for the tree, and another with a pledge to plant it on the homeowner's lawn. One year Hogg learned that the crape myrtles had all gone to white property owners, so he immediately ordered several thousand more trees to be distributed exclusively in black neighborhoods. Today, in older sections of the city, many of Will Hogg's crape myrtles are still flourishing.

In the late 1920s it was Will Hogg who organized the Houston Forum of Civics "to make this city more enjoyable, more adequately equipped, more beautiful," and it was Will Hogg, as chairman of the City Planning Commission, who wrote, "When we build let us build forever. Let it not be for the present delight nor for the present use alone. Let it be such work that our descendants will thank us for, and let us think, as we lay stone on stone, that a time is to come that these stone walls will be held sacred because our hands have touched them and that men will say, as they look upon our labor and the wrought substance of them, 'See! This our fathers did for us.' "

The Hoggs' father had done something for them, too: he left them not only a sense of the public good but the means to implement it. As the 1920s ended, oil was flowing in from the field at West Columbia; Hogg Brothers, Inc., was firmly established; and Will, Ima, Mike, and Tom were learning, in their respective ways, how to use the family fortune. Will was deep in plans for civic improvement and philanthropic ventures; Ima, recovered from her illness, was back into Houston Symphony activities and was beginning to collect antiques (from the acquisition of the very first piece she had planned to build a museum collection); Mike Hogg had entered politics and was serving in the Texas Legislature, following in his father's footsteps as a champion of the public good; Tom, the rebel, was reconciled with his siblings and was raising horses in San Antonio. All things considered, the Hogg family, like most other families in the booming and prosperous 1920s, looked to the next decade with high hopes. The 1930s, however, would bring some unlooked-for changes—both to the Hoggs and to the country.

The Hogg Family

Governor James Stephen Hogg, 1851–1906

Ima gave this turn-of-the-century photograph to her friend in 1975.

William Clifford Hogg, 1875–1930

Michael Stephen Hogg, 1885–1941

Thomas Elisha Hogg, 1887–1949

The Philadelphia Hall in Bayou Bend

Ima Hogg, in 1950, age 68

5

Bayou Bend

When Will Hogg went to Europe in the 1920s and saw St. Peter's Basilica, he decided that its surroundings were not grand enough for it, and he was seized by an impulse to redesign Rome: "It's a positive loss to the world-at-large that St. Peter's does not have a fitting approach," he fumed. A year before his death, he put up $5,000 to start a plan to remove all the houses and public buildings on the way to St. Peter's and replace them with a series of esplanades and parks. Had he lived long enough — who knows? — this larger-than-life Texan might even have left his stamp on the Eternal City. As it was, Will Hogg had only Houston to work with, and he made the most of that.

Houston in the 1920s was already a fast-growing young metropolis whose population had tripled since 1900. There were over 250,000 Houstonians by the middle of the 1920s, and by 1930 there would be nearly 300,000. Houston had newfangled dial telephones, automatic traffic signals, mounted policemen, 34 parks, 233 miles of "hard-surfaced" streets, and other urban amenities such as KPRC, the first commercial radio station in the city, the new Museum of Fine Arts, and a $400,000 sports stadium — but there was no such thing as city planning.

Will Hogg, however, was making his own plans. In 1925 he organized the West End Improvement Association, a center for city planning and "civic forethought." The original headquarters was a little brick schoolhouse on the edge of town, far out Westheimer Road. (The site, no longer so isolated, is the present home of the River Oaks Garden Club.) Later it became the headquarters for the Houston Forum of Civics, whose object was "the improvement of the community in its physical, social, educational or economic aspects . . . to make this city more enjoyable, more adequately equipped, more beautiful — and consequently more useful for everyone who lives and works therein." For a time Will Hogg financed a magazine, *Civics for*

Houston, and published *The Garden Book of Houston,* an expensive color-illustrated work in a ten-thousand-copy edition that he had distributed — free. The Forum of Civics had a library of books on "civic & gardening projects" and a three-hundred-seat auditorium available free to any group dedicated to civic betterment.

In 1927 Mayor Oscar Holcombe finally organized a City Planning Commission, and there was just one obvious choice to head it: Will Hogg. He plunged enthusiastically into this new task, drawing up a list of goals that included a civic center, improved parks and parkways, and a "fool-proof and sensible city zoning plan." But then as now, Houston remained resistant to any zoning plan, sensible or not. Mayor Holcombe himself moved too slowly in support of Hogg's schemes, and when election time came around in 1928, Will Hogg roundly condemned the mayor for his lack of interest in civic planning — and went ahead on his own. The *Houston Gargoyle,* a short-lived weekly magazine of the late 1920s, once called Will Hogg the Superintendent o' Nobody's Business. "He'd see things that everybody was sorry about, but nobody did anything about, an' he'd do something." Largely because of Will Hogg, present-day Houston has a downtown civic center, a huge municipal park, and one of the finest planned residential communities in the nation.

In the mid-1920s Will Hogg bought a tract of land on the then-undeveloped northwest side of the downtown business district, paying over $260,000 for it. The land would be the perfect spot, he thought, for a civic center — something that any city worthy of the name should have. In 1927 he spent $1,000 for advertisements in the Houston papers to support a bond election for civic improvements, including the purchase of the land for a civic center. The bond issue won, Hogg sold the land to the city, and the area is now occupied by the City Hall, the Jesse H. Jones Hall for the Performing Arts, the Sam Houston Coliseum, the Albert Thomas Convention Center, the Music Hall, and the public library.

In 1924 Will bought 875 acres of land on Buffalo Bayou for $175 an acre, later adding 600 more acres at $600 an acre, thinking it would be a perfect spot for a wooded city park. Through an arrangement with the city government, Hogg Brothers, Inc., sold the land to the city of Houston for $650,000, arranging to carry the note for ten years and donating $50,000 to enable the city to make the first payment. This land is now Memorial Park, named by Will Hogg in honor of the dead in World War I.

At the same time that Hogg Brothers, Inc., was buying the land for Memorial Park, Will Hogg, along with Hugh Potter, his college roommate, and his brother Mike, bought 1,100 acres of undeveloped land about three miles west of downtown. This was to become River Oaks, Houston's most elegant residential area. In the 1920s Houston's elite had begun to build their homes just north of the new Rice University campus, in an area known as Shadyside, and farther to the west, in what is now Broadacres. Will Hogg himself was ready to build a home, but he had ruled out living in Shadyside. As architect John F. Staub recalled the story, Hogg had had a "falling-out" with oilman J. S. Cullinan, who already had a house in Shadyside. So Hogg, with characteristic flamboyance, decided to develop Houston in another direction, and he spent $3 million to do it.

River Oaks, first known as Country Club Estates, was modeled after other posh residential areas then springing up across the country: Kansas City's Country Club district, Baltimore's Roland Park, Cleveland's Shaker Heights. Houston's new subdivision was to be a residential park, a haven for affluent homeowners in a growing city of 250,000 people and no zoning regulations. Far ahead of their time in urban planning, the Hogg brothers and Hugh Potter drew up the plans — wide, winding streets intersected by only three cross-streets, a place of trees and grassy spaces, parks and cul-de-sacs, with all utility wires laid underground. All house plans and sales were to be approved by board members of the River Oaks Property Owners' Association. (A "gentleman's agreement" effectively kept out Jews and blacks.) There was even a set of requirements for the discreet placement of garbage cans and clotheslines.

Ground was broken on River Oaks Boulevard, the first street in the new subdivision, in July 1924. At the north end was — and still is — the River Oaks Country Club. The street today is an oak-lined avenue of imposing mansions, but in 1924 River Oaks Boulevard was just a bare road across a prairie nearly four miles from downtown Houston. Nearby, live oaks and loblolly pines towered above jungles of underbrush where wild violets still bloomed and an occasional copperhead crawled. Until the 1920s the area had been farming and grazing land. When the first homesites were offered for sale, the mud was so deep that the developers ordered two truckloads of rubber boots so that prospective buyers could inspect the property without ruining their shoes. Lots ranged from a modest 64 feet by 140 feet for $2,000 to twelve- and fourteen-acre estates with majestic price tags. Will Hogg announced that the country club members would have first crack at the new property and gave them sixty days to choose their lots. "After that," he said, "I'll buy the rest."

Ads in Houston papers enticed prospective customers. An advertisement in the *Chronicle* on January 23, 1925, promised that River Oaks would become a veritable wildlife sanctuary, one "that will not be polluted with gasoline fumes and the feathered and furry creatures will not be frightened by the roar of motor cars." Another ad in a Houston magazine stated that River Oaks would become "the meeting place of an intelligent, refined and chivalrous society." Will and Mike Hogg and Hugh Potter gave a dinner for a group of the new property owners at the Rice Roof, a supper club atop the Rice Hotel, and Will Hogg announced that John Staub, a young architect recently arrived from New York, Birdsall Briscoe, and J. W. Northrop were ready to design some houses for him "on speculation." The first one, built in 1925 at 3376 Inwood Drive, became the W. L. Clayton house. There were regulations, however, about the types of houses that could be built, and as time passed a panel of architects and citizens had to approve each style. Houses that cost under $7,000 could not be built in River Oaks, and on Kirby Drive, one of the main thoroughfares, only English Tudor and American Colonial styles of architecture were allowed.

River Oaks would eventually have some 1,500 homes of varying styles and sizes ranging from modest two-story Cape Cod cottages to lavish Regency, Spanish Colonial, and Georgian mansions and Mediterranean-style villas. Many of the River Oaks houses were designed by John Staub (who, at a sprightly and dapper eighty-nine, attended a round of festivities in Houston in 1979, the year before he died, to celebrate the publication of *The Architecture of John F. Staub: Houston and the South*, by Howard Barnstone). The wealthy owners of River Oaks houses indulged their taste for luxuries — an Olympic-sized swimming pool paved with imported Italian mosaic tiles here, a stair rail fashioned of Lalique crystal to match a chandelier there. Here lived the legendary oil tycoon Jim "Silver Dollar" West, business wizard Hugh Roy Cullen, cotton king W. L. Clayton, and other founders of Houston fortunes. Today River Oaks numbers among its residents other celebrities as well: Gene Tierney, Alan Shepard, Oveta Culp Hobby, John Connally, and Denton Cooley, to name but a few. More than half a century after its creation, River Oaks is still the prime residential area of Houston. Some lots that sold for $9,000 in the 1920s were worth more than $150,000 by the 1970s, and a four-acre tract in the Homewoods section near Bayou Bend sold for over half a million dollars.

It was on the largest of the River Oaks lots, fourteen and a half acres, that Bayou Bend, the Hoggs' home, was built. At her brothers' request, Ima Hogg had been consulting with architect Staub about the designs of some of the houses he was building for the new subdivision, and early in 1927 she said to him, "Do *my* house." The original arrangement was for Staub to work with Birdsall Briscoe, who had been doing some restoration work for the Hoggs on the old antebellum house at the Varner plantation, but as Staub recalled, Briscoe got busy with plans for the house for David Picton, Will Hogg's attorney, who had bought the lot next to the Hogg lot in Homewoods, and so it was John Staub and Ima Hogg who built Bayou Bend.

In the early 1970s, nearly fifty years after the construction of Bayou Bend, Ima Hogg and John Staub reminisced together about the building of the house. She claimed that she drew the first plans of the house and gave them to Staub to execute, but Staub maintained that he never saw any such plans, and that he drew the first sketches and showed them to *her.* Ima Hogg was willing to compromise. Said she:

> I'd made up my mind that there was a certain type of house that belonged in this climate and I got some ideas from New Orleans, because I thought that'd look pretty here. And then I also remembered in Greece where they have brilliant sunlight. . . . All the Greek architecture, you know, was . . . pale pink. It was— every bit of it, pale pink. And I thought, well, now, that's ideal for this sunny climate. So then John and I got together, and we drew some sketches . . .

The house at 2940 Lazy Lane in Houston, with its twenty-two elegant rooms and its acres of elaborate gardens, is far removed from the small frame house in Mineola where Ima Hogg was born. Although Bayou Bend was built as a residence for the bachelor brothers, Will and Mike, as well as for their sister, the house is a reflection of Ima Hogg's taste and judgment. It was she who named it Bayou Bend for the curve of Buffalo Bayou, the lazy brown stream that borders the property on two sides. It was she who helped design the house itself, an imposing structure built of pink-toned stucco. (The original color was achieved by mixing crushed pink quartz with the stucco, but time has faded the color, and in 1979 the house was repainted a pale birthday-cake pink.) The style is vaguely Georgian, with a suggestion of Spanish Colonial influence in the wrought-iron work on a balcony. When the house was being built, Staub dubbed the style Latin Colonial. Hidden from the street and approached by a gently winding, tree-shaded driveway from Lazy Lane on the south, the house has another, more impressive view from the north side, where a reflection pool and formal gardens slope down to the banks of the bayou.

Ima Hogg

Wrought-iron lacework from New Orleans adorns an upstairs porch, and two identical wings flanking the central structure give the facade a graceful symmetry.

John Staub, himself a fancier of antiques, worked closely with his client to design interiors for Bayou Bend that set off her growing collection of Early American furnishings. There were special touches: the woodwork and mantel from eighteenth-century houses in Salem and Ipswich, Massachusetts, graced Ima Hogg's private sitting room and bedroom. The floors were wide hand-hewn planks brought from other old houses on the eastern seaboard. (Ima Hogg arrived at the construction site one day and was horrified to find a carpenter busily splitting the floorboards lengthwise, "so they would look better," he said.) Much of the woodwork in Bayou Bend's rooms was handcrafted and painted to resemble that in colonial American houses. The pale green paneling of the Newport Room, for example, is an exact replica of the woodwork in a room in the historic Hunter House in Newport, Rhode Island. (Four cherub faces carved in the corners of one wall's panels were later whimsically named by Ima Hogg for four of her close friends in the world of antiques: collectors Katharine Prentis Murphy, Henry Flynt, Henry Francis du Pont, and Winterthur expert John Graham.) It was John Staub who chose the vivid blue color for the woodwork and paneling in the east wing sitting room downstairs. Painted in 1928, the woodwork in that room has never needed repainting, and the richly colored panels now form the backdrop for the Queen Anne and Chippendale furniture in the Massachusetts Room, sometimes called the Blue Room.

In the east wing of the house, Will and Mike Hogg had their bachelor quarters, complete with a kitchen, a library, a "tap room," and a small gymnasium. Their sister's rooms were upstairs in the central section of the house, above the drawing room, entrance hall, and dining room on the ground floor. The west wing contained a guest suite upstairs and the main kitchen and rooms for servants downstairs.

In the late spring of 1928 the house was finished, and the Hogg brothers and their sister moved from the house at 4410 Rossmoyne in the Montrose area to 2940 Lazy Lane in River Oaks. Ima Hogg had been in constant attendance during the completion of the house, growing more enthusiastic as the finishing touches were added. John Staub recalled that when plans for the house were first being drawn up, she had seemed in rather delicate health, and for a time she took little interest in the project. As the house progressed, however, so did her involvement, her stamina, and her health. (This was a pattern that was to be characteristic of Ima Hogg throughout her long life. Without a project, she seemed to languish; with a new interest, and a goal to be achieved, she worked with formidable drive and energy.) The finished house reflected countless hours she had spent making small decisions about the color of a hallway or the style of a doorknob. At the last moment, for example, she had changed the plumbing fixtures in an upstairs bathroom to black — a striking complement to the black tiles in the floor pattern. Earlier she had bowed to her brother Will's wishes about the size of the bathrooms in the house. They are unusually spacious. Said Will Hogg, who generally weighed well over two hundred pounds, "I've been in too many hotel bathrooms that were so small you had to *back out* of them to turn around! In this house, I want mine *big!*" It was Will who made another change in the house plans: he would have none of his sister's idea for steps leading down from the living room into the library. Said he, "Do that, and somebody will break their neck!"

While modern conveniences and practical comforts were not neglected, Ima Hogg made sure that Bayou Bend had the ambience of an older, more leisurely era. Thomas Jefferson, the master of Monticello, would have been charmed by Bayou Bend, and Scarlett O'Hara would have felt right at home. The house has a timeless grace about it. Inside the front door a wide central hall spans the house from front to back in the traditional Southern style of the days before electric fans and air conditioning, when houses were built with breezeways designed to capture the slightest air currents in the long, hot summers. To one side of the hallway is the curving oak staircase, reminiscent of the one that Ima Hogg and her brothers used to slide down in the Governor's Mansion in Austin. Presiding over one end of the hall is the portrait of Governor James Stephen Hogg — a solemn, portly gentleman whose imposing presence is a deterrent, if such were needed, to any sliding down *this* banister. Standing in the front doorway, one can look through the glass-paneled rear door to the gardens beyond, to the play of the fountain in the reflection pool and the sweep of green lawn where azaleas and laurels, wax ligustrum and dogwood, gardenias and yew trees and dozens of other plantings grace the grounds in formal patterns. The gardens at Bayou Bend were Ima's doing. They were to become for her a favorite pastime, a never-ending project. In later years, friends would complain that they could never reach her by telephone in the mornings; she was always out with the gardeners, working.

The years that the house was under construction, 1927 and 1928, were busy ones for the Hoggs. In the spring of 1927 Mike Hogg ran for the Texas House of Representatives in a special election to fill a seat left vacant by Judge Norman Kittrell of Harris County. Since World War I he had been an active participant in the business affairs of Hogg Brothers, Inc., sharing the sumptuous offices atop the Hogg Building with his older brother. He had finished law school in 1911 at the University of Texas and had spent some time as a law clerk for the firm of Gill, Jones, and Stone, the firm founded by his father and formerly known as Hogg, Gill, and Jones. Will described his younger brother in those years as "not particularly studious" but "fairly aggressive and industrious." Now, at age forty, Mike Hogg was about to enter politics, following in his father's footsteps.

James Stephen Hogg had been dead for more than twenty years, but there were many people still around to remember him and to vote for his son. Supported by the *Houston Chronicle*, Mike won the election and went off to Austin. He soon made something of a name for himself in the legislature, speaking eloquently and defending the "little people" against big business just as his father had done. When a bill to allow the building of oil pipelines for offshore loading of tankers came before the Texas House in 1927, Mike argued against it on two counts: by allowing ships to take on oil in the open seas, it would deprive Texas ports of a source of revenue in port charges, but more important, said Mike Hogg, undersea pipelines would pose the risk of serious pollution of the Gulf Coast's waters. Speaking in the legislature, Hogg developed the habit of punctuating his speeches with an emphatic "by golly," which reminded observers of his father's famous "by gatlins." In 1928 Mike ran again for the same seat in the regular election, and he won.

Busy with affairs of state, he had a house in Austin and spent little time in the new home at 2940 Lazy Lane in Houston. But in the summer of 1929 bachelor Mike Hogg married an attractive young divorcée, Alice Nicholson Frazer of Dallas. Oddly enough, Ima was out of the country when the wedding took place. She and Eloise Chalmers, a former piano student who became one of her closest friends, had left in June for an extended trip to Europe and Russia; Mike and Alice were wed in Galveston in July. Ima did not return until October. But the siblings remained close, and by 1931 Alice and Mike were living next door to Bayou Bend, in the house at 2950 Lazy Lane. Alice and Ima, the sisters-in-law, were to become good friends, and often worked together on various civic projects, especially the River Oaks Garden Club.

Will Hogg, meanwhile, had been appointed to a second term on the University of Texas Board of Regents (he had served an earlier term from 1914 to 1917) and was busy with the newly created City Planning Commission in Houston. Will, like his brother Mike, was to spend little time in the family's new home. In the summer of 1928 he went to Europe, and he left Houston again in December of that year for an extended trip to South America with his friend Irvin S. Cobb, the author and humorist. He did not return to Bayou Bend until March 1929, and he was off again in the spring of 1930 for another long European holiday.

Perhaps these extended trips gave him some respite from worries about Tom, his youngest brother, who, at forty-two, was still as irresponsible and extravagant as ever. Tom tried periodically to be frugal, but his budget always seemed to be out of hand. In the spring of 1929 Blanche Hearne, his secretary and business manager in San Antonio, wrote to Will that she was planning to "have a nice talk with him and try to make him see where it is wrong to hide bills and notes as he has for the past few months." In 1930, while Will was in Europe, Tom wrote an enthusiastic letter to his brother. The letter, dated March 29, was written in Tom's usual breezy style. He discussed Will's recent weight loss and his own health: "Am delighted to know you are under 180 for the past six weeks. . . . My average weight is 182 to 185. Am hard as a rock and brown as a peon." The Hogg brothers all had their father's tendency to excess weight, and all of them tried periodically to slim down. Tom had even entered a hospital in San Antonio to undergo a controlled weight reduction plan. He had written jubilantly to Will in July 1929 that he was "down to 216, which is 32 lbs off in six weeks." Will had answered ruefully, "I am at least 25 pounds heavier than I have ever been." But by the time of his trip to Europe in the spring of 1930 Will had lost nearly fifty pounds. Such a dramatic weight loss suggests that he was not in the best of health, whether he realized it or not. The remainder of his youngest brother's letter did not make him feel any better. It was full of Tom's prospects for horse breeding and his plans to take ten or fifteen of his horses to shows in Chicago and St. Louis in the fall. In a penciled scrawl across the top of the letter, however, is the notation "MH would like to keep him out of shows if could." What Tom Hogg wrote about in the last part of this letter is not known: the last two thirds of the second page have been neatly cut off.

Tom Hogg was himself apparently cut off from the Hogg Brothers, Inc., funds for a time. In August 1930 Blanche Hearne wrote again to the Hogg office in Houston, with details of Tom's continued extravagances and news of a bank overdraft: "It will do him more good to be hard up for a while, and if the Bank is willing to carry him, I think you will agree it is one way to hold him down, for a few days at any rate. . . . If one could just convince him he had enough horses." What Will Hogg's response to this situation would have been, one can only guess. He never saw the letter.

Still vacationing in Europe, where he had been since the spring, Will had been joined by Ima, and the two were at the Badhof Hotel in Baden-Baden, Germany, when Will was taken seriously ill with a gall bladder attack. He had emergency surgery, but he died in Germany on September 12, 1930. Once again, Ima Hogg had to cope with the death of a loved one. It was she who sent the cablegrams back to Texas; it was she who accompanied the body on its last ocean journey, back to New York. A funeral service was held there, and then another service in Houston. Among Will Hogg's pallbearers were Irvin S. Cobb, columnist O. O. McIntyre, and Colonel Edward M. House.

Will Hogg left an estate of over $2 million, but he had already given away more than $1 million to various educational institutions, including his beloved University of Texas, and probably some $2 million to other philanthropic projects during his lifetime. Said his close friend John Lomax, "Not even his family can tell what he gave away privately." Will Hogg, who shunned publicity all his life, was eulogized far and wide at his death. Roscoe Wright, editor of the *Houston Gargoyle*, wrote a piece called "Tender Tempest — A Tardy Tribute to Will C. Hogg," in which he described Hogg as "this keen, contradictory, fiery, generous man. . . . This tender tempest." While he lived, Will's efforts to avoid being praised for his good deeds were legendary. When the Museum of Fine Arts wanted to honor his fund-raising efforts with a reception, he heard about it and left town. When a group of prominent Houstonians scheduled a surprise presentation of a medal for his distinguished services to the people of Houston, he feigned illness, went home from his office early, and spent the evening in bed. When the Rotary Club gave him its award for civic service, said Roscoe Wright, "he wouldn't come and get it. Never went to luncheon clubs. They had to go up to his office and pin it on him." Will once threatened his friend O. O. McIntyre, "If you put my name in your column of tripe, I'll kick you so hard you'll taste leather the rest of your life." But after Will's death there was no one around to prevent the tributes from being paid. Ima Hogg filled a scrapbook with clippings of eulogies to her brother. In 1933, the Museum of Fine Arts dedicated a commemorative tablet in his honor.

It was a few years after Will's death that the editor of *Atlantic Monthly* asked John Lomax to do a biographical sketch of Will Hogg for a series the magazine was running on picturesque Americans. Lomax wrote to the people who had known Will Hogg, and they responded. His friend Guy McLaughlin wrote, "The item one remembers first and most vividly were those blue eyes, their depths particularly, and their twinkle when amusement charged them with additional snap." Martin M. Crane, who had been a state senator during Jim Hogg's terms as governor, wrote at length to Lomax but cautioned him to avoid things that might give offense to Ima, Mike, and Tom. Lomax duly consulted the family, but apparently there was some misunderstanding about the result. Ima Hogg wrote an indignant letter to Lomax demanding to see the finished piece before it went to press: "I was disappointed and surprised," she wrote, "when I found you had sent your article on to the editor, Mr. Weeks, without letting Mike or me see it or advising us of its contents — as you had promised." She advised Lomax that she was sending a copy of her letter to Weeks. Weeks then sent the galley proofs of the article to Ima Hogg, with the stipulation that only single sentences could be changed at such a late date, and he sent a terse telegram to Lomax informing him of what had been done. Apparently few, if any, changes were necessary, and Ima Hogg made no mention of any in her appreciative note to Lomax after the article appeared in the May 1940 issue of *Atlantic Monthly*.

After Will's death in 1930, Ima Hogg was alone in the big house on Lazy Lane. She had servants, including her devoted personal maid, Gertrude Vaughn, who had been with her since 1919 and would be there the rest of her life. Mike and Alice Hogg lived in the house next door; Tom and Marie Hogg continued their carefree existence on Tom's Varner Hills Farm in San Antonio. Her brothers, however, would not be a part of Ima Hogg's life much longer. In 1940 Mike Hogg — Mickey, as she called him — died at his home after a two-year struggle with cancer. He was fifty-six years old. Alice, his widow, remained close to her sister-in-law, but she would remarry, becoming Alice Hanszen in 1948. Little is known about Tom, the youngest of the Hogg brothers, in this period. In 1940 he left San Antonio for Kerrville, and in 1942, after the death of Marie, he lived for a time with Ima at Bayou Bend. In 1945 he married again, and he and his wife, Margaret Wells Hogg, divided their time between Houston and Yuma, Arizona. But in 1949 Tom, too, was gone. He died in Arizona at age sixty-one. Ima Hogg would outlive her siblings by more than a quarter of a century.

As the 1930s began, Ima, who had lived most of her life in the shadow of her older brother, taking his advice, catering to his whims,

Ima Hogg

and obeying his commands, was on her own. At forty-eight, she was no longer young, but middle age became her. Her hair was still blonde, her complexion smooth and fair, and though she was no longer slender, she carried herself regally and dressed exquisitely. As the years passed her diminutive figure inclined to plumpness, and she, like her brothers, had to watch her weight. Photographs of her show a handsome woman, and there is a hint of firmness about the mouth, a slightly determined air. The private griefs, the periods of depression she had suffered as a young woman, were behind her, and for the next forty years Ima Hogg gave the outward impression, at least, of one who had taken control of her own life and enjoyed it to the fullest.

There would be occasional bouts with depression, but she battled them with such quiet courage that few people knew about them. She traveled, she collected art and antiques, she resumed her active role in the affairs of the Houston Symphony, she worked at various civic projects, she even took up her music again. In 1932 she played a concert at Bayou Bend. Houston music teacher Adele Margulies presented Ima Hogg in a program of selections that drew a favorable response from a *Houston Post* critic: "Playing in a manner that lifted her performance to the level of a real artist, Miss Ima Hogg was presented in a piano recital . . ." She played the Chopin Nocturne, Opus 37, No. 2, with "firmness and strength," and in the rest of the pieces, ranging from Debussy to a Bach organ prelude, the reviewer praised her "clarity and delicateness of phrasing." Although this recital was well received, Ima Hogg did not intend to make music her career. She had given that idea up long ago, and this concert was perhaps an effort to prove to herself that she could still give a creditable performance as an artist. She saved the clippings of the newspaper review, carefully preserving them along with the dozens of other clippings she habitually cut out and kept.

There is a collection of clippings dating from the 1930s in the Hogg papers in the University of Texas archives, and their range reveals the variety of Ima Hogg's interests as she reached her fifties: notices of concerts by other pianists, a recipe for fudge and maple candy, an account of the Harvard–University of Texas football game (Harvard won 35–7), a travel piece about driving to Mexico City, an article about Mahatma Gandhi's rules for living, a *New York Sun* series about Germany's recovery from World War I. One wonders what prompted her to cut out the articles on Germany — was it perhaps the memory of the smiling young man in that long-ago photograph? Whatever the reason, in her fifties she was apparently as resolute in her decision to remain single as she had been in her twenties. Although she once told a friend that she had received over thirty proposals of marriage during her lifetime, she "wouldn't have any of them." But it was not that Ima Hogg did not like the company of men; in fact, she seemed to prefer male companionship to that of her own sex. She dealt well with men, perhaps because she had dealt well with her father and her three brothers for so many years.

On one occasion, when Joseph S. Smith had retired from the presidency of the Houston Symphony and a replacement had to be found quickly, Ima Hogg summoned eight prominent Houston men to tea at Bayou Bend. When each man arrived, she slipped him a confidential note that said, "You have been nominated to be the president of the Houston Symphony Society." She then saw to it that her guests received some refreshments: "tea" turned out to be bourbon old-fashioneds, served in silver tumblers. When everyone was present, she called the meeting to order to discuss the crucial lack of a symphony president — and revealed the note trick, observing wryly that each man there had managed to whisper to her his pressing reasons for not being able to accept the presidency. Amid the general laughter, one of the group, Walter H. Walne, was finally prevailed upon to accept the post, which he held for the next four years.

In 1946, when Hugh Roy Cullen, oil tycoon and chairman of the symphony's board of directors, opposed a move to replace conductor Ernst Hoffman and ousted Joseph Smith, who was then serving a second term as Symphony Society president, it was Ima Hogg who hurried back from a vacation in Mexico to bring peace to the warring factions. Unfazed by Cullen's explosive temperament, she arranged a confrontation — but she took along protection in the person of financier Gus Wortham, who had been a longtime close friend of hers. The outcome was something of a Pyrrhic victory for Ima Hogg. Cullen, who had threatened at one point to remove his considerable financial backing from the symphony, was mollified enough to agree to rethink his decision, but only on one condition: Miss Ima herself must consent to become the next symphony president. She did. Many years earlier, from 1919 until 1921, when her illness had forced her to leave the affairs of the orchestra to others, she had served as the president of the Houston Symphony Society. This time she would hold that position for ten years, until 1956.

The Houston Symphony was among Ima Hogg's prime concerns for over half a century, but it was far from being her only interest. In 1928, with the building of Bayou Bend, she had ended almost a decade of intermittent ill health and reclusiveness with a burst of activity. In the spring of 1929 she went on an extended trip to Europe, going first to France, then touring Sweden and Denmark, and venturing into Soviet Russia with a group of Americans on an educational tour. In Moscow, Ima Hogg visited the Museum of Modern Art, and began to think of collecting contemporary paintings as well as American antiques. It was on this trip that she bought a painting by Paul Klee and two Picassos.

Although she was abroad from May to October 1929, Ima Hogg found time that year to help establish the Houston Child Guidance Clinic, a center for the study and care of mentally disturbed or "difficult" children. Eventually there would be training programs for parents and teachers of such children, psychological counseling services, and in later years a special school. Some forty years later, Ima Hogg declared that it was this project — of all her many projects — that had given her the most pleasure. She had her own reasons, perhaps, for a consuming interest in mental health. Besides her own experience, there was her youngest brother, Tom, who had been something of a problem child after their mother's death. He was only eight at the time of Sallie Hogg's death in 1895, and despite thirteen-year-old Ima's attempts to comfort him, he had gone through a difficult period of adjustment. At boarding school at Lawrenceville, New Jersey, a few years later, he did poorly. As an adult, Tom was a constant source of worry to the rest of the family — restless, impulsive, and alarmingly careless with money. Ima Hogg once told a friend that "if only poor little Tom" had had the counseling services of an agency like the Child Guidance Clinic in his early years, he might have turned out differently.

Ima Hogg's interest in mental health did not end with the clinic. After her brother Will's death in 1930 she began to consider establishing some kind of memorial to him, and in 1940 the Hogg Foundation for Mental Health was created at Will's alma mater, the University of Texas. Working closely with Dr. Robert Sutherland, the first director, Ima Hogg created an agency that would not only conduct research into mental health problems but would design programs to promote mental health as well. One of the first projects sponsored by the Hogg Foundation was a lecture series to carry the newest ideas about mental health and modern psychology to rural Texas towns.

While plans for the Hogg Foundation were under way, Ima began to think of appropriate ways to pay tribute to another Hogg whose memory was even dearer to her than that of her brother Will. James Stephen Hogg was never far from his daughter's thoughts. In 1933 she gathered his letters to her and her brothers, had them all typed and bound into a volume that she called simply *Family Letters*, and gave them to Mike and Tom at Christmas. She took up the research on the Hogg family history that she had once begun some years before, and she began gathering information about her father's political career, carrying on a correspondence with people who knew him. She wrote to T. N. Jones, a Tyler, Texas, schoolteacher who had been one of her father's key campaign workers in the bitter election of 1892. She asked former state senator Martin M. Crane to reminisce about James Stephen Hogg, and she also corresponded with H. B. Marsh, one of her father's law partners. It was about this time that she wrote to historian Herbert Gambrell about her father, and it was not long afterward that she began to work with another historian, Robert C. Cotner, on a volume of her father's papers and speeches. Later Cotner, working closely with Ima Hogg, would write his ponderous, adulatory biography of James Stephen Hogg. It depended heavily on the reminiscences of the governor's only daughter. Cotner, of course, had the use of the Hogg papers in the University of Texas archives, but his research was clearly influenced by the fact that Ima Hogg was almost literally looking over his shoulder most of the time. From Ima came the explanation of how she was named; from Ima came denials of Hogg's crude but picturesque political manners; and it was Ima who said that William Jennings Bryan would have made her father his secretary of state if he had won the presidency in 1900.

Ima was the self-appointed guardian of James Stephen Hogg's place in history — a task that seemed to call for extraordinary vigilance. People were always saying things about him that Ima considered untrue, and more than once she rushed into print with a counterstatement or a denial. There was the story of his drinking out of the water pitchers on speaker's platforms, mentioned earlier, and there were, from time to time, stories about Ima's name. She always denied — vehemently — that her father ever joked about her name and that he ever pretended she had a sister Ura. But hearsay and legend have it otherwise, and folk memory is sometimes based on fact. There are some old-timers in East Texas who claim they heard him say it. However, the very fact that Ima had been burdened with a name that made a lifetime of explanations necessary also made her anxious to defend her father from all detractors. By doing so, she defended herself as well, and she did so with considerable skill and unfailing politeness.

Ima Hogg, the governor's daughter and the state legislator's sister, made her only venture into politics after their deaths. In 1943 she ran for and won a seat on the Houston school board. Before that, she had always maintained, as she said in 1974, "I *am* interested in politics . . . but I don't *do* anything about it." A lifelong Democrat

Ima Hogg

(how could Jim Hogg's daughter be anything else?), she did defect from party ranks in 1940, when she voted for Wendell Willkie, and in 1952, when she was for Eisenhower. In 1940 her brother Mike had been a Willkie supporter, and he even prevailed upon his shy sister to make a brief radio speech on CBS, urging Texans to vote for Willkie. In state and local politics, however, Ima Hogg was a loyal Democrat. Despite her claim that she didn't "do anything" about politics, she did more than most people. She contributed to various campaign funds, she wrote letters to the editor about various issues, and she voted faithfully in every election that came along.

When the Houston school board race came along, Ima was persuaded to run for Position 3 against two male candidates. As she put it later, "In a weak moment, at the request of the Citizens' Educational Committee, I filed for the School Board election." Ima Hogg was never a militant feminist, but in this case she felt that the seven-member Board of Education ought to have some women on it. Another woman, Dr. Ray Daily, an ophthalmologist, was running for one of the other positions. Of her principal opponent, Dr. C. M. Taylor, a dentist, Ima Hogg said: "If he had been a woman I would have been supporting him instead of running against him. I made the race because I felt the board should have two woman members." The *Houston Press*, which ran an editorial in her support, said: "Miss Hogg is no politician, and all her talents and efforts during her lifetime have been devoted to unselfish, public-spirited work for the betterment of social conditions or for the improvement and enrichment of life for others." There is a certain irony in the fact that the daughter of one of the canniest politicians in Texas history made political capital out of not being a politician. Said Ima in a campaign speech on March 28, 1943: "It is a matter of principle with me not to curry favor by making pre-election promises." She won by a comfortable margin: when the votes were in, T. A. Lambright had 109, Dr. Taylor had 3,026, and Ima Hogg had 4,350.

Once on the board, she found the inevitable divisions among the members "disheartening." "Sometimes," she said, "I am sorely tempted to resign from the School Board, for I really don't think I'm suited for that kind of public service. It is too involved with extraneous influences. But then I visit the schools and feel reassured." During the campaign she had promised nothing; once in office, however, she produced results. Drawing on her work with the Child Guidance Clinic, she helped to establish a visiting teacher program for emotionally disturbed children who could not fit into the regular routine of daily classes, and she worked to equalize the salaries for all teachers—for elementary school and high school, for blacks and whites, for men and women, correcting a salary scale that had long been in need of reform. True to her own artistic interests, and determined that school should enrich the spirit as well as enlighten the mind, she worked to establish a painting-to-music program in the district's art classes, and she saw to it that the then-segregated high schools provided art instruction for both blacks and whites. Using her influence with the Houston Symphony (she was then on the Women's Committee), she established a series of symphony concerts for Houston school-children — a practice that is still carried on today. Since the 1940s the student matinees have introduced thousands of children to the world of classical music. But for Ima Hogg, many of those young people would never have seen the inside of a concert hall or heard a live symphony orchestra.

In the 1940s Ima Hogg was more active in civic and philanthropic affairs than she had ever been. These were the war years, and in 1943 a 10,500-ton Liberty ship built in the Houston shipyards was named for Ima Hogg's father. She was asked to christen the ship, attending the launching festivities with Alice Hogg, Mike's widow. With Will and Mike both gone, Ima had pondered what to do with the collection of Remington paintings that had hung in the offices atop the Hogg Building, and in 1943, after consultation with Tom, she presented the entire collection of fifty-three oils, ten watercolors, and the bronze *Bronco Buster* to the Museum of Fine Arts. Besides her work on the school board in these years, Ima served as one of the leaders of the Community Chest; she worked with the River Oaks Garden Club, the Child Guidance Clinic, the newly created Hogg Foundation, and, as always, the Houston Symphony.

Tom M. Johnson, general manager of the orchestra from 1948 to 1973, never forgot his first encounter with Ima Hogg. They met in Austin, where he had a position with the Austin symphony orchestra. Ima Hogg, a regal presence in a hotel lobby, informed Johnson that a city the size of Austin did not need a professional symphony orchestra, and a civic organization could serve quite well. It was clear to Tom Johnson that Ima Hogg, a founder of the Houston Symphony, would brook no competition from upstart orchestras. Shortly afterward, Johnson came to Houston and took his post as manager, much to Miss Ima's satisfaction.

In later years she was fond of attending the orchestra's Sunday morning rehearsals, but she was never one to interfere in the artistic side. It was the "bottom line" that concerned her most, and she did her utmost to see that the symphony's financial affairs were kept in good order. Once, working to whittle down a deficit, she raised $7,500 in pledges in twenty minutes at a symphony meeting. On another occasion, determined to reach Houston for an important board meeting and delayed in Williamsburg, Virginia, by a spring rainstorm that flooded the airport, she waded through knee-deep water to board her flight to Houston. She was then in her seventies.

Her devotion to the cultural life of Houston is reflected in her remarks at a ceremony in 1956, when a scholarship in her name was established by the Symphony Society: "If we are musical and artistic, and it seems we are, we shall cultivate our taste. If we are neither of these, we shall not shirk our duty in altering that deficiency." A grateful symphony organization dedicated the opening concerts of October 1956 to Ima Hogg as she retired from the presidency.

The Houston Symphony would grow under Tom Johnson's management, and by 1955 there was even a Houston Grand Opera, but Ima Hogg's favorite city still had some growing up to do. The 1946 *Life* magazine feature story called "Booming Houston" observed that although the Bayou City was growing fast (the postwar population was 675,000), "bumptious Houston still shows signs of immaturity." By the mid-1940s there was an international airport terminal (travel time from Houston to New York was eleven and a half hours; transatlantic flights were nearly twice that), and in 1948, the city's first commercial TV station, KLEE, would begin broadcasting. But according to *Life*, people in Houston still liked to sit in their cars along Main Street on Saturday nights to watch the crowds downtown, and in this city of nearly 700,000, people read only 100,000 books a year from the public library.

The *Life* magazine piece was not altogether complimentary to Houston, but it labeled Ima Hogg Houston's social leader. She was then sixty-four years old. At an age when most people begin to slow down and think about retirement, Ima Hogg, living alone at Bayou Bend, was just coming into her own.

6

The Collector

In 1950 an article about Houston in the magazine *People Today* described Ima Hogg as "a little 67-year-old woman with light brown hair and twinkling eyes" who was the "spark-plug of the city's cultural life." Ima Hogg, in her sixties, was busier and perhaps happier than she had ever been in her life. It was as though, with Tom's death in 1949, the constraints of family connections and responsibilities were removed, and she was free at last to be herself. Houston author George Fuermann wrote of her in his book on the history of the Bayou City: "She is a woman of great personal charm and a paradox of the practical and the intellectual." In 1956, Ima Hogg, then seventy-four, served her last term as president of the Houston Symphony Society, but she was far from finished as the guiding spirit and *grande dame* of that organization, and her role in the city's cultural life had barely begun.

Like her brother Will, Ima Hogg kept a watchful eye on the progress of Houston, which was by the mid-twentieth century a bustling, booming, hustling, adolescent city whose city fathers had never bothered much with guiding its growth. When there was talk of building a municipal stadium on part of the Memorial Park land, Ima Hogg (who, along with her sister-in-law Alice Hanszen, owned three quarters of the reversionary rights to that land) wrote a polite but firm letter of opposition to the Houston newspapers. A few years later, in 1964, she had to protect Memorial Park again, when the city proposed drilling for oil under the leafy glades by the bayou. Both then and after the energy crisis of the early 1970s, Ima Hogg had to threaten to take back the park land to keep it from becoming an oil field adjacent to River Oaks. She was always keenly interested in the environment, just as her father and brothers had been. Perhaps the memories of the Piney Woods of East Texas and the rolling, tree-shaded hills of turn-of-the-century Austin, where she played as a child, reinforced her determination to keep Memorial Park unspoiled for the children of Houston. In the mid-1960s, when flood control authorities proposed cutting down a number of hundred-year-old live oaks on the banks of Buffalo Bayou and lining part of the rustic stream with concrete, Ima Hogg and some forty other property owners along the bayou protested loudly enough to halt that project.

When Will Hogg died in 1930, Houston had nearly 300,000 people; thirty years later it had a population of one million and the downtown area was fast becoming a forest of skyscrapers. In 1961 Ima Hogg, along with cotton magnate W. L. Clayton, endorsed the work of a commission that had developed plans to convert the old City Hall Square in downtown Houston to a landscaped mall with an underground parking area. The site is now Tranquility Park, a pleasant oasis amid the concrete and chrome of downtown Houston. When the old City Auditorium was torn down in 1963 to make way for the construction of the present Jones Hall, there was no place for the weekly wrestling matches to be held, and it was Ima Hogg who led the protests against putting them in the nearby Music Hall — then Houston's only major concert hall and the home for many years of the Houston Symphony and Houston Grand Opera. In January 1963, in the midst of a spirited debate and exchange of newspaper letters between the "highbrows" who wanted the Music Hall for cultural events only and the "lowbrows" who wanted a home for their wrestling bouts, Ima Hogg sent a telegram to the mayor and offered to contribute to a fund to build a new hall for the wrestling matches. That sport finally found a home in the Coliseum, where it has remained ever since.

Throughout the 1950s and the 1960s, when Ima Hogg was in her seventies and eighties, she took a lively interest in public affairs, and more than most people, she did something about them. She wrote letters to editors; she wrote to her congressmen. In 1959, for example, she sent letters to Lyndon Johnson and Tom Connally, asking the two Texas senators to suggest that President Eisenhower proclaim a day of prayer for world peace during Soviet premier Nikita Khrushchev's visit to the United States. The public schools, she thought, could hold special ceremonies, and churches could have prayer services. She was an active member of civic organizations ranging from the Community Chest to the River Oaks Garden Club to the League of Women Voters, and in 1956 she helped to found the Harris County Heritage and Conservation Society, beginning the historic preservation project that created Sam Houston Park, a collection of antebellum and Victorian houses set in a grassy sloping park at the edge of downtown Houston. As a member of the Texas State Historical Survey Committee, Ima

Hogg continued her interest and expanded her knowledge of historic preservation. Sentimentally attached to the Governor's Mansion in Austin, she served on an advisory board to maintain it, and she gave it a set of antique parlor furniture made by John Henry Belter, one of the most highly regarded craftsmen in the late nineteenth century. By the mid-1950s Ima Hogg was working with Robert Cotner on the biography of her father, spending long hours in interviews and traveling with him through the governor's old haunts in East and Central Texas. In December 1956 she spoke at the dedication of the new quarters for the Hogg Foundation for Mental Health on the University of Texas campus, and she presented the director, Robert Sutherland, with a book her father had owned: *Responsibility in Mental Disease,* published in 1878.

It was not long after this that Ima Hogg conceived the idea of writing a memoir of her childhood years as the governor's daughter, and while she was collecting material for that, she kept a critical eye on the works of others who wrote about James Stephen Hogg. But sometimes she was too late. Author Harvey Katz, in a 1972 book on Texas politics called *Shadow on the Alamo,* wrote that "Hogg won the election of 1892, but he stained the ballot box with murder, fraud, and the most terrible atrocities. While he was in office, Jim Hogg became exceedingly wealthy. He certainly remains the most notable sell-out in Texas history." Hogg's daughter was understandably furious. She took some satisfaction when a *Houston Post* story drew attention to Katz's inaccuracies, including his statements about Governor Hogg.

She was more successful in preserving and protecting her father's memory in other ways, such as the restoration of the old family home at the Varner plantation, the excavation and reconstruction of his birthplace at Rusk, and the creation of a museum at Quitman. The most ambitious of these was the project at Varner, begun after Will Hogg's death and completed in 1958. The house where Ima Hogg had lived as a young girl at the turn of the century was in need of major repairs, and Ima pondered what to do. Since the deaths of her brothers she had seldom visited the old plantation, but the place held too many memories for her ever to consider selling it. Finally she decided not just to repair the house but to restore it and give the building and some of the surrounding land on the banks of Varner Creek to the State of Texas for a park. This was to be her first, and certainly not her last, effort at historic preservation. The Varner plantation was, after all, a spot rich in historic interest, having been one of the original land grants issued to settlers who came to Texas with Stephen F. Austin in the 1820s. A man named Martin Varner had been the original owner, receiving number nineteen of the first three hundred grants issued to prospective colonists by the Mexican government in 1824. Varner received 4,500 acres of fertile South Texas land on the banks of a creek, a tributary of the Brazos River. There he built a small two-room cabin near the creek bank, raised sugar cane, and made the first rum manufactured in Texas.

In 1834 Varner sold the plantation to Columbus R. Patton, who built a much larger house around Varner's cabin, even making use of some of the cabin's sturdy fourteen-inch-thick log walls as part of the first-floor structure. The house, modeled after a Virginia plantation style, was built by slaves with bricks made of pink clay from the banks of the Brazos River. The main entrance of the house faced the small tree-shaded stream known as Varner Creek. Small boats could make their way up and down this stream to the Brazos River and from there into the Gulf of Mexico, providing the plantation with its easiest link to the outside world. Travel by water, in those days of rutted, muddy, sometimes impassable and always bone-jolting roads, was viewed as a decided advantage.

The plantation house, built with thick walls and high ceilings, was well suited to the sultry summers of the Gulf Coast. The windows were large, designed to catch every breeze, and every room in the house had cross-ventilation. A large central hall connected the front door and the back door, with a parlor on one side and a bedroom on the other. The kitchen, as was the custom in many Southern houses, was nearby in a separate building, to keep the heat from the wood stove out of the rest of the house. Upstairs, in a repetition of the first-floor plan, another central hall served as a breezeway and was flanked on either side by a large bedroom with windows on three walls. The Patton family lived in this house until after the Civil War, when, in 1869, they sold the plantation.

The old Varner place, as it was still called, changed hands several more times before James Stephen Hogg bought it in 1901. He had been looking for a place to make a family home for his children. Will was by that time a young lawyer of twenty-six; Ima, nineteen, was studying music in New York, and the two younger boys, Mike and Tom, sixteen and fourteen, were away at boarding school. There was no real "home place" for them during holidays and summer vacations, and Jim Hogg, cherishing childhood memories of Mountain Home, the big plantation in East Texas that his father's family had lost after the Civil War, wanted a place where his own family could gather. He also wanted a place where he could amuse himself with one of his favorite hobbies: horticulture. While he lived at Varner there were watermelons and peaches in profusion, as well as tomatoes and beans and squash and every other kind of vegetable from his gardens.

In her nineties, Ima Hogg recalled with great fondness and clarity the turn-of-the-century summers she had spent at Varner:

> That was very, very lovely. We enjoyed it so much. We had a lot of pets down there. We had horses. We used to go hunting at night — coon hunting. Oh, yes! I had a wonderful horse. He was an Arabian horse, and he was the most intelligent animal. I never saw anybody so clever. There was a little creek we had to cross when we were riding after the coons. Every time we'd get in the creek he'd turn around and look at me, and turn over! It wasn't deep, but he'd turn around and look at me and turn up his nose. Then he'd get up and let me get on his back again! The fishing was wonderful, too. We had a lake near there — Maynor Lake, they called it, a great lake for fishing. We'd go up there in these little flat-bottomed boats, and catch fish, and fry the fish right there on the bank. I think they were mostly perch. They were very good. I don't think they had any trout. I don't remember any, but little perch about *that* long — very, very good. I don't think they were muddy, although the lake was full of pads — lily pads. I don't know how deep it was. We were in those flat-bottomed boats. Oh, we had a grand time down there! We were off at school most of the time, and we'd come back there. And we had visitors. We didn't have very many rooms there, either, and the bathroom was on the end of the porch, and there was a tank right by the bathroom, and we had to pump the water in, and if we had hot water, we had to bring it upstairs from the kitchen!

It is somehow difficult to imagine the *grande dame* of Houston's cultural circles as she was in her Varner plantation days — a lithe young girl riding horseback helter-skelter through thickets and across creeks on a moonlit night in pursuit of a pack of "coon dogs" who in turn pursued the quarry, a raccoon. She was always fond of horses, and she was perhaps a better rider than her brothers: when the governor of Tennessee gave Jim Hogg a handsome white horse in 1899, Hogg allowed Ima, but not her brothers, to ride it. She could also shoot. In 1902 Will, trying to entice her to Varner when she was studying music in New York, wrote to her that if she would come home, she could "shoot a duck or two." On evenings at Varner when there was no hunting or fish frying, there might be music in the parlor, where Ima would play on the elaborately carved upright piano that had been hers since the age of ten.

After Jim Hogg's death in 1906 the family went less and less often to Varner, and the house was closed for a time. It had been James Stephen Hogg's favorite place, and it was not the same without him. His children had another reason, however, to be concerned with Varner: oil. Their father had always suspected that some day the 4,100 acres that he had bought for $7 an acre might be valuable for what lay under them. In 1919 oil was discovered at the Varner plantation, and the next year Will and Mike, in consultation with Ima and Tom, who were both away, began extensive renovations and remodeling of the house. They removed the old second-floor gallery from the front of the house and added six square white columns to make a two-story veranda. The old dining room was enlarged and a breezeway connecting it to the parlor was added. The kitchen was remodeled, but the giant old wood-burning stove was left in place. The antique brick exterior of the entire structure was covered with white stucco.

As the 1920s progressed, however, the Hoggs' energies and interests lay farther and farther from the tree-shaded banks of Varner Creek. Will Hogg increasingly spent his time at his Park Avenue apartment in New York, filling it with antiques and art treasures, and Ima, by 1927, was engrossed in the plans for building Bayou Bend. Through the years, however, she managed to furnish the house at Varner with antebellum pieces and family mementos. Among the antiques at Varner were a black horsehair parlor set — settee and chairs — that had belonged to the Hogg family in Austin and a white homespun bed coverlet made by Ima Hogg's maternal grandmother from cotton grown on a family plantation in Georgia around the time of the Civil War. After Mike Hogg married and moved out of the "bachelor quarters" at Bayou Bend in 1929 and Will Hogg died a year later, their sister moved some of their furniture to Varner.

The restoration of the house at Varner and the collection of furniture for it took place over a number of years, however, and was not completed until the late 1950s. As Ima Hogg described those years in an interview in 1974:

> I restored my father's home, down at Varner. I couldn't restore it, actually, because there had already been things done to it. My oldest brother wanted to enlarge it and do different things to it. The interior is original. The exterior is not like it was. . . . [The house] tells the story of Texas. You go to the first

hall, and that is the colony. To the right is the Confederate . . . and the left room downstairs is our forefathers. Then you go upstairs, and in the middle hall, memorabilia of my father, and then on the right side — there was an attempt, oh, way back about 1818 — when the followers of Napoleon wanted to set up an empire and they came here. They thought they'd get him out of prison, and they'd bring him here and set up another empire . . . and that is that room. Then the left room is a family room. There were many people that lived there, and we had things from everybody . . . different things. And the dining room is Mexican War, and all the things from that, and the kitchen is just "done over." It *is* a pretty kitchen. And the smokehouse is still there, and the pantry has a lot of china — very interesting, old-fashioned china.

Today visitors to Varner-Hogg Plantation State Park approach the house by a short curving driveway shaded with oak and pecan trees. Spanish moss hangs from the massive old oaks, just as it did a hundred years ago. Close to the house, twenty large magnolia trees, planted by the Hogg family, form a neat rectangular border for the front lawn. In the spring the heavy sweet fragrance of their white blossoms perfumes the breeze. (When Ima Hogg planned her funeral, she wanted nothing but magnolias for the floral spray on her casket.)

Ima Hogg's gift to the people of her state is rich in Texas history. The house is a museum of Texana from the early days of the Austin land grants in the 1820s to Jim Hogg's governorship in the 1890s. Portraits of Stephen F. Austin, Sam Houston, Zachary Taylor, and Jefferson Davis adorn the walls. Framed copies of the original land grant to Martin Varner in 1824 and the deed to the property given to Columbus Patton in 1834 testify to the original ownership of Varner. Upstairs in the central hallway are James Stephen Hogg's memorabilia: photos and papers from 1891 through 1895, his terms as governor of Texas; his massive oak rolltop desk and swivel chair, and his collection of walking sticks. By a window is a handsome oak rocking chair, one of the many made by state prison inmates during the Hogg administration. The chairs were a product of the prison workshops and were sold all over Texas as "Jim Hogg porch rockers." On one wall there is a touching reminder of Ima Hogg's relationship with her father: a small, delicate drawing of a shepherd boy, done by a thirteen-year-old Ima and given to Jim Hogg on his birthday in 1895 — the year his wife, Sallie, died of tuberculosis.

In the East Bedroom, which was once Ima's room, there is a cedar canopy bed made in 1845 by Henry Adolphus Jansen, a Texas crafts-man who worked in the nearby town of East Columbia. Ima Hogg tried to find regional furniture made near the houses or buildings she was restoring; when that proved impossible she sought out pieces made in the same period of history as her restorations. In the West Bedroom, which is devoted to the Napoleonic era, there are two an-tique beds made from the mahogany banisters of a staircase in the old St. Louis Hotel in New Orleans. The washstand, bureau, and dressing table were made by Prudent Mallard, a cabinetmaker in antebellum New Orleans. These New Orleans pieces might well have been in the houses where Napolean's supporters plotted to bring him to America.

Downstairs and across the breezeway, the dining room is furnished with pieces from the 1840s — the Mexican War years. Much of the fur-niture here, including a mahogany pedestal dining table, was also made in New Orleans. The table is set with Staffordshire Texian Cam-paigne china, made in England to commemorate the Mexican War and sold in the American market in the 1840s and 1850s. On the walls of the dining room, some of the battle scenes on the plates are repeated in a collection of early lithographs.

In the adjacent smokehouse, used by the Hogg family as a sort of pantry, Ima Hogg used Early American furnishings, mostly maple and pine "country" pieces, some made in colonial America more than two centuries ago. Many of these furnishings were collected by Will. The eighteenth-century Windsor chairs around the table are still sturdy, joined without glue or nails. The dining table is a "dough table" made with a long shelf underneath to hold rising bread. The table is set for dinner with early eighteenth-century American-made knives and forks and English plates. On the cupboard nearby are pewter lamps de-signed to burn whale oil. The kitchen adjoining the smokehouse re-mains much as it was when the Hoggs restored the room in 1921, with its enormous wood-burning stove and cavernous fireplace faced with the original 1835 slave-made bricks. Antique kitchen utensils and cop-per pans hang above a cutting table in the center of the room. Every-thing lies ready for use; all that is lacking is a fire in the stove and the makings of a meal.

Ima Hogg's painstaking restoration of the Varner-Hogg plantation house was her first effort at creating a museum, but it certainly would not be her last. By 1958 she had already decided that Bayou Bend would become a museum, and no doubt as she worked at Varner she had visions of the rooms she would create at Bayou Bend. About the Varner place, as she was about everything else, Ima Hogg was metic-ulous and exacting. In 1955, a few years before the plantation was dedicated as a state park, the *Dallas Morning News* carried an article by Texas historian Frank Tolbert about the tiny community of West Columbia. Tolbert, a first-class scholar as well as a spinner of tales about early Texas, had in his article one bit of misinformation. He described the old Varner house as having been built in 1836. Ima Hogg was quick to correct him. In a letter to the newspaper she politely set the facts straight: Columbus Patton had bought the place in 1834, not 1836. Long after the Varner-Hogg place had become a state park, Ima Hogg looked after it. When Hurricane Carla was roaring toward the Texas Gulf Coast in 1961, Ima Hogg telephoned the caretaker and reminded him to make sure the windows on the south side (toward the hurricane) were securely boarded up.

Perhaps it was only natural that Ima Hogg, with a mind as keen and curious as any historian's and an eye for style and detail as discerning as any artist's, would develop a passion for collecting antiques. It had all begun after that long bout with depression in 1920, when Will Hogg had encouraged his sister to take an interest in collecting during her convalescence in the East. Will helped, but it was Ima who had the inspiration to collect only American-made furniture and art. At the time she made that decision, only a handful of collectors in the country were interested in Early American pieces.

When Ima Hogg began to collect, American pieces were seldom recognized as having any value. To most collectors and dealers, antiques were by definition European: Louis XIV chairs, Renaissance tables, Georgian silver, were what was wanted. American furniture and decorative arts were too recent and too familiar to the generation of World War I, and they rejected as out of fashion the handcrafted highboys and secretaries and tea tables from their grandparents' houses and filled their own homes with new tables and sofas and whatnots done in the curving lines of Art Nouveau or the "modern" angles of Art Deco. And so American-made pieces in old houses in New England and elsewhere were consigned to attics or handed down as makeshifts to newlyweds waiting to afford their own new furnishings.

If Ima Hogg read the December 1920 issue of *House Beautiful*, she saw an article entitled "Furnishing a Home with Antiques," which told its readers, "There is nothing wrong with old things, which can be picked up for a few dollars at an auction." The tone was faintly apologetic; the prices quoted were indicative of the values that era placed on "old things": six solid silver teaspoons for $1.50, a mahogany side table for another $1.50, a secretary for $5. In 1929, however, a *Ladies' Home Journal* article inquired, "Is the Antique

Fever Waning?" In the decade before the Great Depression, antique hunting had become a more fashionable pastime, and prices for American pieces had risen accordingly. At one auction in Doylestown, Pennsylvania, for example, a Queen Anne maple side chair went for $280 and comb-back Windsor chair for $775. These were high prices at a time when one could buy a new Model T Ford for under $300.

In Texas, however, almost no one but Ima Hogg was collecting American antiques. It was only in the eastern United States that some awareness of the value of American pieces was growing, mainly because that area was where most of the old furnishings had remained. Furniture made by early American craftsmen was often relegated to storerooms or attics, where Ima Hogg and other collectors learned about them. A fine old Chippendale mahogany lowboy, for example, made in Philadelphia around 1770, stood for many years in the basement of the First Congregational Church in Seattle, where the Ladies' Aid Society attached a towel rack to its side and used it for a washstand until 1946. It was then discovered quite by accident, by a lawyer who found it listed in a client's will as "the old wash stand in the basement of the Congregational Church." Divested of its washbasin, pitcher, and towel rack, the lowboy was sent back east to a dealer in Philadelphia, where Ima Hogg bought it in 1948.

In the drawing room at Bayou Bend there is a massive secretary carved from solid mahogany, made in Massachusetts around 1760. Little is known of its early history until 1818, when it was auctioned off for $25 to a Cape Cod schoolmaster because it was, according to an ink inscription inside one of its drawers, "rather ancient and out of fashion." Ima Hogg, who had been doing her homework, knew better, and added the piece to the Bayou Bend Collection — for a sum considerably higher than $25. An imposing eighteenth-century highboy in the central hall at Bayou Bend was once listed in a nineteenth-century estate inventory as a "chest with 12 drawers" and assigned a value of $15. A century later the highboy was offered for sale at a price almost two hundred times that amount. As the twentieth century progressed, the value of American antiques escalated and brought prices undreamed of in the early years of collecting. In 1971, for example, the first price tag over $100,000 for an American piece was placed on a Rhode Island–made highboy sold to tobacco heiress Doris Duke. Collecting antiques has never been a pastime for penny pinchers.

It is not surprising that the pioneer collectors in America happened to be from families with distinguished names and great fortunes: Ford, Rockefeller, du Pont. By the 1920s these aristocrats of American industry were spending part of their money to preserve the preindustrial past, and their creations were an added inspiration to Ima Hogg. As Henry Ford's Model T and Model A cars rolled off the assembly lines, he began to put some of his wealth into historical restoration and antique collecting. He was the first great pioneer American collector and preservationist, and the first project he undertook was the restoration of his own birthplace, the original Ford family homestead in rural Dearborn, Michigan. Born there in 1863, Ford began restoring the place in 1919. After that project would come others: Longfellow's Wayside Inn in 1923, the old Botsford Inn near Detroit in 1924, and finally the crowning achievement, the Henry Ford Museum and historic Greenfield Village at Dearborn. About the same time that Ford's efforts were generating a new interest in the American past, another and perhaps a more famous restoration was undertaken: Williamsburg, Virginia, the old colonial capital of the first English colony in America, was to be returned to its original state with the help of another famous American family's fortunes. John D. Rockefeller, Jr., son of the oil tycoon, was persuaded in 1926 by the Reverend William A. R. Goodwin, rector of the old Bruton Parish Church at Williamsburg, to fund a restoration project that took decades to complete and now draws thousands of tourists and scholars every year.

One of the greatest of all the collectors of the 1920s was Henry Francis du Pont, grandson and heir of Henry "the Red" du Pont, who in the last half of the nineteenth century had masterminded the fortunes of the gunpowder dynasty in Delaware and made that family one of the richest in America. This first Henry du Pont had also bought Winterthur, an estate near the Brandywine River, for his family home. After his grandson inherited the property in 1926, he set about remodeling it by installing rooms taken from eighteenth-century houses around the countryside and filling them with colonial American furniture and artifacts, and the work of this Henry du Pont was to have a profound influence on Ima Hogg and the creation of the Bayou Bend Collection. In 1924 the American Wing of the Metropolitan Museum of Art opened in New York. This was the first comprehensive collection of period American rooms in any museum besides the Essex Institute at Salem, Massachusetts, where some alcoves of American colonial furnishings had existed since 1907. Ima Hogg immediately sought out Charles Cornelius, the first curator of the American collections at the Metropolitan, and he eventually became her good friend and adviser, as did his successors, Joseph Downs and Vincent Andrus.

By the 1940s American collecting and museum making, which had

103

come to a virtual halt during the ravages of the Great Depression and the austerity of the Second World War, had become fashionable once more, and Ima Hogg had to compete with other collectors who were buying American antiques. In 1947, in Shelburne, Vermont, Electra (Mrs. J. Watson) Webb began a preservation project that would turn into a twenty-acre plot with nearly thirty colonial buildings furnished with seventeenth- and eighteenth-century American artifacts. One of her houses, an old saltbox house from North Hadley, Massachusetts, was furnished with antiques by another collector, Katharine Prentis Murphy, who, like Electra Webb, began actively collecting American antiques in the 1940s. Katharine Murphy furnished and donated an impressive number of seventeenth- and eighteenth-century rooms to the New York Historical Society, the Shelburne Museum in Vermont, the New Hampshire Historical Society, and Columbia University. "Individuals do not own these things," Mrs. Murphy once said. "They belong to the people." Deerfield, Massachusetts, is a village that now belongs to the people because of another collector's fascination with the American colonial past. In the late 1940s Mr. and Mrs. Henry Flynt set out to restore and preserve Deerfield, a New England frontier community that dates from the seventeenth century. For many years the Flynts devoted their efforts to collecting and preserving the artifacts and the furnishings of colonial life in restored and reconstructed buildings at Deerfield, and Henry Flynt and his wife, Helen, became good friends of Ima Hogg's.

With few exceptions the major collectors — Ford, du Pont, Flynt, Webb, Murphy, and others — were in the North and the Northeast. Ima Hogg, living in Texas, hundreds of miles from antique auctions and dealers' showrooms, was far from the mainstream of collecting.

In the 1920s Ima had begun to study what there was to know about the American decorative arts in the colonial period. There was not much at first. In 1922 Alice Winchester, who was to become a good friend of Ima Hogg's in later years, began to edit a monthly magazine called *Antiques*. It is now the bible of antique fanciers all over the country. When the first issue of *Antiques* appeared, however, the study of Early American art and artifacts was still in its infancy. Not until 1952 would the Winterthur Museum, in cooperation with the University of Delaware, establish a graduate study program and a center for art historians and American studies experts.

Given the relative lack of expert knowledge about her chosen field, Ima Hogg, a beginner at collecting, proceeded with extreme caution. In 1922 she visited Luke Vincent Lockwood, whose *Colonial Furniture in America* was the standard work on Early American antiques.

The Collector

Lockwood himself was a collector, and his Riverside, Connecticut, house was full of pieces that Ima admired. After her visit she wrote to the Lockwoods, thanking them for their hospitality and saying that if they ever chose to part with any of their collection she hoped they would let her know. The Lockwoods were not disposed to sell, and it was not until some thirty years later, when Lockwood's collection was sold at auction after his death, that Ima Hogg bought some of his pieces for Bayou Bend.

In 1928, while Bayou Bend was still under construction and she and her brothers were living on Rossmoyne, Ima acquired two pieces that she had read about and seen illustrated in Lockwood's book, which Will had sent her in 1921: a Queen Anne highboy and a tray-top tea table, both made about 1740 in Connecticut. In later years she would acquire some of the other items pictured in Lockwood, including one of the earliest pieces of American furniture extant — a carved-oak chest made in the 1680s. Ima Hogg not only studied; she took notes and kept meticulous records of her findings. In the files at Bayou Bend, for example, is a slip of paper with detailed notes in her handwriting describing the cornice of the Queen Anne highboy, and a citation of the volume and page number of Lockwood's book as carefully documented as any scholar's footnote. On the same slip of paper is a further note recording where she put the highboy: a penciled note indicates "W.C.H. bedroom," but that has been crossed out and underneath it is written, "Mickey's Room."

In the late 1970s, New York antiques dealer Bernard Levy reminisced about Ima Hogg: "at the beginning she wasn't as knowledgeable and experienced . . . and she did not react to material the way a knowledgeable collector would. Her reactions were more social. . . . After that she became more seriously interested, and as the thought of developing a museum developed, she wanted the best." Another dealer, Harold Sack, remembered Ima Hogg as a hard trader in later years. Once when he sent her a photograph of an eighteenth-century Baltimore secretary, she wrote back immediately, asking, "Why is the satinwood of the plinth a different color from the wood on the frieze?" "And do you know," said Sack, "she was right! It *was* a different color, and nobody up here had noticed it at all."

While Ima Hogg was never one to let a choice item get away if she could help it, she was also mindful of how she spent her money. Bernard Levy remembers that when he first met her in the 1930s he had the impression that she was "terribly wealthy, but her first purchases were dictated by how inexpensive the items would be, and her continual crying that she didn't have the funds." William Ferguson, her attorney and the chief financial adviser to the Hogg family for over fifty years, recalled that she handled her own finances where the purchase of antiques was concerned. "The only advice I ever gave her," said Ferguson, "was 'Give now. Don't wait till you're dead.' And she didn't wait." In the 1950s, partly for tax reasons, Ima Hogg gave certain pieces in her collection to the Museum of Fine Arts, but she kept them at Bayou Bend.

It was in the 1950s that Ima Hogg met the collector who would become one of her closest friends: Katharine Prentis Murphy. Mrs. Murphy was by then a well-known New England collector. Said Ima Hogg: "Many of the dealers used to tell me about Mrs. Murphy, and I was afraid of her. I thought she would be a very awesome personage." She was. Her collections were in museums all over the Northeast; her closets were full of clothes designed by Givenchy. In character Katharine Prentis Murphy was, as one friend said, "a regular Auntie Mame." Ima Hogg and her party, traveling through New England, were supposed to arrive at Mrs. Murphy's Westfield, Connecticut, home in time for afternoon tea. They had stopped to see a dealer on the way, however, and then had taken a wrong road. They did not arrive until nearly nine o'clock in the evening. After greetings and apologies had been exchanged, Mrs. Murphy inquired of her guest whether she would like a drink.

"Oh, yes," said Miss Ima gratefully, "I'd like a martini."

"Well, then," said Mrs. Murphy coldly, "make it yourself!"

After the initial chill of that first encounter, the two became close friends. Said Ima Hogg of Katharine Murphy, "I found that she was the most wonderful, cordial, enthusiastic person; we became immediate friends." Said Mrs. Murphy of Miss Hogg: "She is the only truly *good* person I've ever met who wasn't *boring!*" So close did the two become, in fact, that for many years they visited regularly on Sundays by telephone. Ima Hogg created and named the seventeenth-century Murphy Room at Bayou Bend for her friend. From a professional point of view, however, Katharine Murphy had little to offer Ima Hogg. Bernard Levy, who knew them both as collectors, once remarked: "Her friendship with Katharine Murphy was a disaster, because while she loved Katharine a great deal, Katharine always suggested that she buy the cheaper rather than the better item. On Katharine's advice she bought a number of wrong or fake items which she later disposed of."

Ima Hogg seldom let sentiment or historical value distort her aesthetic judgment, however, and she bought with an eye to line, form, and craftsmanship first and history second. In the Newport

Room at Bayou Bend is a silver sugar bowl made by Paul Revere around the time of the Stamp Act riots in Boston in 1765 and owned for generations by one of the oldest and most distinguished families in that city. Ima Hogg nonetheless made certain the sugar bowl was in near-mint condition before she agreed to buy it. A descendant of the Winslow and Hutchinson families offered the bowl to her in 1956 and recounted its distinguished history: The bowl had belonged to Elizabeth Hutchinson Winslow, wife of a Mayflower descendant and granddaughter of a famous religious rebel, Anne Hutchinson, who was banished to Rhode Island in 1638. Elizabeth Winslow was a cousin of another famous Hutchinson, Thomas, the Loyalist sympathizer and lieutenant governor of revolutionary Massachusetts. These illustrious connections did not impress Ima Hogg, who wrote to the sugar bowl's owner, "I would be interested in the bowl if it is in good condition without any dents in it. Of course, the sentiment of the bowl would mean something, but I like for all the pieces in my collection to be in good condition. If not, I would not want to consider it."

Ima Hogg was equally cautious about another piece with impressive historical credentials: a silver tankard made by Jeremiah Dummer, the earliest native American craftsman whose silver and pewter pieces are extant and identified. This particular tankard was once owned by John and Experience Swain of Nantucket, Massachusetts. The couple might well have drunk a toast in it to celebrate the birth in 1706 of a nephew, Benjamin Franklin. Franklin's mother, Abiah Folger Franklin, was the sister of Experience Folger Swain. Experience and John had a daughter, Hannah, who inherited the tankard sometime after her marriage to Thomas Gardner, and the tankard was then passed down through five more generations of Gardners, whose initials and dates of acquisition are engraved on the base of the tankard: THG–1740, TAG–1784, CAG–1817, ESG–1847, EB*MG–1875, ECSG–1905. When the last inheritor, Edmund Gardner of New York, died without an heir, his widow approached Vincent Andrus, then curator of the American Wing at the Metropolitan Museum, about finding a home for the Dummer tankard. Andrus, a friend of Ima Hogg's, mentioned it to her, and she then corresponded at some length with Mrs. Gardner, visited her and viewed the tankard in New York, bought it, and in the end invited Mrs. Gardner to visit her in Houston at Bayou Bend.

In 1955 Ima Hogg carried on another lengthy correspondence from June to November with dealer John Walton about a japanned chest in the Harrison Gray Otis house in Boston. She wanted the piece, a rare example of the mid-eighteenth-century technique of imitating oriental lacquer designs by copying Chinese pagodas, animals, and other figures in gilt paint over a surface painted to resemble tortoiseshell. There are only two other chests of this type known to exist: one is at Winterthur and the other is at the Metropolitan Museum.

Ima Hogg was concerned at first about the authenticity of the japanning work on the chest, and was suspicious that it had been restored at some later date — which would enhance its appearance but decrease its value as an antique. The chest had belonged for a time to the Society for the Preservation of New England Antiquities, which acquired it from the family of a Mr. Frank Brewster in 1935. In the society's records, however, was a disturbing note: "This cabinet repaired and redecorated Jan. 1900, Joseph Norton, decorative artist, with J. H. Boody, Brookline." But by the 1950s, no one knew who Norton and Boody were. The information could not be verified, and Ima Hogg, after much deliberation, finally wrote to John Walton:

> My dear Mr. Walton:
> I don't think I am going to worry any more about the lacquered highboy. I like it very much and shall just content myself with whatever restorations that seem to have been made on it. With kind regards,
>
> > Sincerely yours,
> > Ima Hogg

It was John Walton, some years later, who bid for and acquired the two pieces — a Massachusetts chest and matching kneehole dressing table — that Ima Hogg had admired so long before at the Luke Lockwood home. The high chest-on-chest and dressing table, made of mahogany and white pine with heavy brass hardware and rare gilt carved fans for decoration, were part of the Lockwood estate sold at auction by Parke-Bernet in 1954. Walton was the highest bidder on that occasion, taking the two pieces for $25,000. Ima Hogg, however, was not completely happy with the price tag. She wrote to Walton: "While I am happy to have the chest on chest and the bureau, frankly, I was a little shocked to hear what had been bid for them." She went on to say that Walton had exceeded the sum she had authorized, and in view of that, she considered his customary ten per cent commission a bit too much. "Would five per cent seem fair under the circumstances? If not — maybe you know someone who would like to have the pieces at your price. Do not misunderstand me. I appreciate your effort and will stand back of your bid if you wish, but I want you to feel satisfied. And I also want to feel able to buy other things later." She was never one to let a dealer have the upper hand.

The Collector

Before the Lockwood estate auctions she instructed her three major dealers — John Walton, Harold Sack, and Bernard Levy — to take care not to bid against each other for pieces that she wanted, such as Mrs. Lockwood's piecrust tea table. At the height of Ima Hogg's collecting, in the 1950s and 1960s, there were perhaps a half-dozen other major collectors in the market, all seeking the finest pieces to put into museums. It was inevitable that they would come into contact — and conflict — with each other. To avoid hard feelings, she often made purchases anonymously. For example, in 1951 there was a rare card table for sale at Ginsburg and Levy, Inc. They sent photographs of it to Ima Hogg and suggested they would be glad to show the table to her if she desired it. The card table, which had once belonged to the wealthy Faneuil family in Boston in the early eighteenth century, was a masterpiece, carved of mahogany, made with a special accordion action that extended the top to full size for gaming, and covered with a colorful, intricately stitched piece of eighteenth-century tambour work. There were many other collectors besides Ima Hogg who would have liked this table, and so she bought it anonymously, giving strict instructions to Ginsburg and Levy not to reveal to anyone who had purchased the famous Faneuil card table. As she triumphantly observed some time later, "I don't know how many hands it passed through, and I bought it, and my dear friend Henry Flynt nearly died because he had been wanting that table." On another occasion when Bernard Levy was preparing to bid for her at an auction of more of Luke Lockwood's collection, she wrote to him: "One thing I didn't mention is that purchases not be made in my name, but that they be *kept in your name.*"

One of the stories that she loved to tell in later years was about her first encounter with Henry Francis du Pont. Du Pont, like Ima Hogg, began collecting seriously in the 1920s, and like her, he bought from the New York dealers Collings and Collings. But he and Miss Ima, though sometimes frequenting the same showrooms, had never met. He kept a standing order with Collings and Collings to notify him immediately when any piece of unusual quality or rarity came into their hands. In 1927 they acquired one of the rarest items in Early American furniture: eight perfectly matched mahogany Chippendale chairs and a matching chair-back settee. Made in Massachusetts sometime between 1760 and 1790, the set was handed down in the Forbes family of Worcester, Massachusetts, from that time until 1855, when they were sold to one G. R. Sandford. His son offered them to Collings and Collings in 1927. On the day the chairs and settee were delivered, Ima Hogg, on one of her trips to New York, happened into the showroom. The Collingses had not yet had time to put the set away for Henry du

Pont's inspection, and she spied them. Remembering the incident nearly fifty years later, she said, "I went in there one day and saw them and said, 'I want that!' and bought them right on the spot. . . . I thought I had paid the most horrible price, but it is nothing. Mr. du Pont came in a little later and was furious." (This, at least, was Ima's recollection in a talk she gave to the Bayou Bend docent class on October 18, 1971. On other occasions, however, she said that her brother Will was the one who made the purchase and that she was appalled at the price he paid for the chairs and the settee. Since none of the parties to this transaction is still living, it is impossible to say which version of the incident is correct.)

Eight matched Chippendale chairs in good condition are themselves a rare find, but with the carved-to-match chair-back settee the set is virtually priceless. No more than five such settees are known to exist. Henry du Pont finally did get one of them for Winterthur, but the matched set remains at Bayou Bend. In the best of households, however, accidents happen. In the files at Bayou Bend is a note from a curator's worksheet on one of these chairs: "Rear stretcher badly chewed (by Miss Hogg's dog)." Actually the culprit was Will Hogg's dog. The chewed chair was consigned to an upstairs hall, and Ima's comments to her brother and his dog have not been preserved. In later years when Henry du Pont and Ima Hogg became good friends, he always referred to the Chippendale chairs and settee as his and demanded to see them when he came to visit Bayou Bend. Said Miss Ima, "That was probably the only thing he wanted that he couldn't buy."

It was not until 1947 that Ima Hogg visited Henry du Pont's home at Winterthur, just outside Wilmington, Delaware. When she saw his impressive collections of American furniture and art for the first time, she was ecstatic. On August 26, 1947, she wrote him a letter expressing her thanks. "My dear Mr. du Pont," she began, "I have no words to express my appreciation for your most gracious hospitality of yesterday at 'Winterthur.' " The handwritten draft of this letter, laden with crossed-out words and phrases, testifies to the care she took in composing it. "What you have done to preserve these noble expressions of our culture is an everlasting treasure for posterity, and it fills the beholder with gratitude that we can have it to see. It strikes one with aesthetic pleasure and patriotic gratification at the same time. . . . Excuse me for being fulsome or trite, but we really haven't recovered from the thrill of the day."

As the years passed, Henry du Pont and Ima Hogg became friendly rivals as collectors. In March 1956 du Pont and his wife, Ruth, came to Houston to attend a Fine Arts Forum sponsored by the Museum of Fine Arts. The du Ponts stayed at the Shamrock Hotel, but Ima Hogg entertained them at Bayou Bend during their visit and gave a cocktail party in their honor on the last day of the forum. About a month before the meeting in Houston, Ruth du Pont had written to Ima asking if there was anyone in the city who knew how to do marcel waves. Ima wrote back: "I shall endeavor to find a marcel artist. Some years ago, I also wore my hair long, without a permanent, and I had one woman who knew how to wave, but that has been 16 years ago. I don't want to depress you about the possibility for I feel sure we can dig up someone." In a postscript to this letter she wrote triumphantly, "I have just learned that the operator at the Harper Method Beauty Shop at the Warwick Hotel (not far from the Shamrock) gives Marcel waves."

A few weeks before the du Ponts were scheduled to arrive in Houston the always-modest Ima wrote to Henry du Pont: "Please don't expect anything much of my collection. You are such a connoisseur it rather frightens me to think of your viewing what I have assembled. Nevertheless, it will be fun to have you in my home." On the occasion of the Fine Arts Forum, she had other collectors in her home besides Henry du Pont. Katharine Prentis Murphy, Electra Webb, and the Ralph Carpenters of Scarsdale and Newport were house guests at Bayou Bend. From Thursday until Sunday there were lectures and seminars for the experts on American decorative arts and antiques. Ralph Carpenter, director of the historic Hunter House in Newport, Rhode Island, and author of two books on Early American furnishings and restorations, was a featured speaker, as was Ima's friend Henry Flynt of Deerfield, Massachusetts. It was a remarkable group of the most influential collectors in the country, and their presence in Houston was largely due to the efforts and the growing reputation of Ima Hogg as a collector. She had been made honorary curator for American art at the Museum of Fine Arts in 1948, and her interest in American furniture and art was becoming known in circles outside the state as well.

Texas in the 1950s, however, was still considered a cultural wasteland by many Easterners. A *Holiday* magazine article in 1957 said that "a state built on crude oil naturally produces a crude society." But if some Texans had not yet acquired the polish and social graces of their Eastern counterparts, at least they tried hard to learn. Some years after that Fine Arts Forum, Ralph Carpenter recalled his first visit to Houston with some amusement: "On the first night we were invited for dinner at the Houston Club. The New England contingent all appeared in black tie, but the Texans were all in business suits. Well, the *next* night the same group was invited to have cocktails at the Harmon Whittingtons' home and then to go on to Bayou Bend for dinner. *That* night the *Texans* were all in black tie, and *we* were all in business suits!" As a Texan dealing with New Yorkers and New Englanders, Ima Hogg had more than just geography to overcome.

By the end of the forum, however, both the Texans and the Easterners were at ease, and the cocktail party at Bayou Bend for the du Ponts was deemed a great success. This occasion had been the du Ponts' first visit to Houston, and it marked the beginning of a friendship with Ima Hogg that would last until Henry du Pont's death in 1969. The mistress of Bayou Bend and the master of Winterthur kept up a constant exchange of letters, gifts, and visits. The du Ponts sent her sugarplums and flowers, including a gardenia plant that she put in her garden and dubbed the "Henry F. du Pont gardenia." She sent them Texas grapefruit and turkey sausage. ("Is there such a thing?" Ruth du Pont wrote to her, thanking her for the "huge and marvelous" sausage and exclaiming, "You are an angel to spoil us so, and you really shouldn't do it!") Ima Hogg also became a good friend of Henry du Pont's sister, Louise du Pont Crowninshield. Mrs. Crowninshield once wrote a letter addressed simply to "Ima Hogg, River Oaks, Houston, Texas." The house at 2940 Lazy Lane, however, would not be Ima Hogg's address much longer.

It was sometime after the Fine Arts Forum that Ima Hogg made the decision to give Bayou Bend itself to the Museum of Fine Arts. Inspired by what Henry du Pont had done at Winterthur, once the du Pont family home, and moved by the need for an appropriate setting for her growing collection, she began the formidable task of converting the house built for the Hoggs in 1928 to a home for the American Decorative Arts Wing of the Museum of Fine Arts, Houston, in 1958.

7

Presents from the Past

Most people would have considered the creation of a museum like Bayou Bend the achievement of a lifetime, but Ima Hogg's interest in preserving the past was not confined merely to collecting American decorative arts. During the years she was building the collections at Bayou Bend she was also engaged in the preservation of her parents' house at Quitman, the excavation of her father's birthplace at Rusk, and the restoration and reconstruction of several antebellum buildings in the old German community of Winedale, near Round Top, Texas. Between the dedication of the Varner-Hogg Plantation State Park in 1958 and the opening of Bayou Bend in 1966 Ima Hogg decided to restore the house where her parents had lived in Quitman, Texas, in the 1870s. The small frame house where James Stephen and Sallie Hogg had set up housekeeping when they were newlyweds was rebuilt, restored, and refurnished. It is now known as the Honeymoon Cottage and is open to visitors. The town of Quitman, where Jim Hogg had spent some of his early years, had honored his memory in 1951, the centennial year of his birth, with a Jim Hogg Day, and in 1969, Quitman paid homage to the governor's daughter with an Ima Hogg Day and the opening of the Ima Hogg Museum on the grounds of the Jim Hogg State Park. At the dedication ceremony, held in the Quitman High School stadium, the band played "Oh, You Beautiful Doll" as the convertible carrying Ima Hogg came onto the field. By then Ima, acknowledging cheers from the crowd, was no stranger to awards and honors. In 1953 Governor Allan Shivers had appointed Ima Hogg to the Texas State Historical Survey Committee, and in

Ima Hogg

1967 that body gave her an award for "meritorious service in historic preservation." In 1960 she found time to serve on a committee appointed by President Dwight Eisenhower for the planning of the National Cultural Center (later Kennedy Center) in Washington, D.C. In 1962, at the request of Jacqueline Kennedy, Ima Hogg served on an advisory committee to aid in the search for historic furniture to put in the White House. During all this time, she was also working long hours on the conversion of Bayou Bend, her home for more than thirty years, to a museum.

Of that period, Ima Hogg said later, "I had an awful time for a while. Everything had its problems." One of the early problems had to do with her neighbors in River Oaks, who objected to the idea of a museum in a private residential neighborhood. It is a testimony to Ima Hogg's powers of persuasion that none of her immediate neighbors in Homewoods voiced any objections at all. But some of the other residents of River Oaks sought court action to prevent the creation of the museum. Miss Ima put the matter in the hands of her attorney, a Houston lawyer named Leon Jaworski, and in 1958 the courts ruled that Bayou Bend could become a museum.

As the Museum of Fine Arts prepared to accept Ima Hogg's gift, along with a $750,000 endowment to provide for maintenance of the collections and the house, there was another problem: what to do about the museum traffic on the quiet streets of River Oaks, and how to provide for parking space. Miss Ima suggested a footbridge over Buffalo Bayou so that visitors could approach the house from Memorial Drive, about half a mile north of the Hogg property, rather than from the winding driveway to the main entrance on Lazy Lane. The City of Houston agreed to build a bridge, and city funds also provided for a parking lot on the west bank of the bayou adjacent to the footbridge. The bridge now provides a picturesque entry to the gardens of Bayou Bend. Made of weathered wooden planks supported by cables from above, it gives gently with the weight of its pedestrian traffic. Underneath, some thirty feet below, is Buffalo Bayou, a muddy, slow-moving stream banked by the lush foliage of laurels, elms, sycamores, and magnolias. Naturalized plantings of monkey grass along the sloping banks have kept the soil from washing into the stream in heavy rains. Ima Hogg wrote in 1961, "Now things move very slowly and we have the additional problem of living on an eroding bayou bank. But that is another story!"

Docents at Bayou Bend still tell the story of the flood of 1933, when Buffalo Bayou rose over its banks in a swirling, threatening torrent and flooded the first floor of Bayou Bend. As the muddy water crept into the house, anxious servants, directed by an imperturbable Ima Hogg, moved priceless furniture and rugs to the second floor. When they asked her whether they should remove the china from the storage cupboards in the pantry, she replied, "Yes, about up to there," indicating a shelf about four feet from the floor. A few hours later the floodwaters in the house rose to that exact level — and stopped. As it happened, she had dreamed a few nights earlier that Bayou Bend had been flooded to precisely that point. For many years the water line could be faintly seen on the walls. Now it has been papered over.

Once the decision to turn Bayou Bend itself into a museum had been made and the bridge and parking lot provided for, Ima Hogg turned to what she called the purification of the house: the eradication of all traces of her personality and the eventual removal of all furnishings other than American antiques. Out went the Picasso above the mantel in the drawing room, out went the two Steinway pianos — a baby grand in her upstairs sitting room and a grand piano downstairs in the drawing room — but in stayed the English pedestal dining table. It should stay where it was, she decided, because of its sentimental value. "I am sure you often wonder why in a collection of American furniture we still have an English dining table," she once told a group of docents.

I am most sentimental about the table, for here have sat dear members of the family and friends, as well as many distinguished collectors. My old collector friends who have visited Bayou Bend, such as Katharine Prentis Murphy, Electra Webb, Helen and Henry Flynt, Miriam Morris, the Ralph Carpenters, Mr. and Mrs. Harry du Pont, have sat around this table, as well as many others. And while I was president of the Houston Symphony Society I entertained at dinner such great men as Igor Stravinsky, Carlos Chavez, Leonard Bernstein, Maurice Abravanel, Georges Enesco, Charles Munch, Efrem Kurtz, Sir Thomas Beecham, Dimitri Mitropoulos, Eugene Ormandy, Leopold Stokowski, Erich Leinsdorf, Andre Kostelanetz Heitor Villa-Lobos, and Sir John and Lady Barbirolli.

Of all the rooms in the house, the dining room underwent the fewest changes in the conversion to a museum. That may be partially due to Ima Hogg's determination to use it for entertaining, even after the house opened to the public as a museum in 1966. After hours, when the iron gate was locked and the docents had gone home, Ima Hogg continued to entertain occasionally at Bayou Bend. She would come from her nearby high-rise apartment to greet guests on the terrace for cocktails while a small army of caterers prepared an elegant dinner for eight or ten. She liked to see her treasures used as they were meant to be, and dinner guests ate with reverence and more than ordinary care from eighteenth-century porcelain and salt-glaze plates and serving dishes. After dinner the remains would be whisked away, the dishes returned to their shelves, and no telltale crumb would be visible next morning when the staff returned.

The dining room today is just as Ima Hogg conceived it in 1927. The woodwork is Adam style, inspired by the molding in an eighteenth-century Charleston house, and the walls are covered with a painted canvas designed and executed by artist William MacKay of New York. On a background of gold leaf, pale green and white Texas dogwood trees bloom and provide a resting place for an occasional butterfly or bird. When the painting was in progress, author-humorist Irvin S. Cobb, a close friend of Will Hogg's, suggested that one of the birds should be a Texas hummingbird. Cobb did the research himself and presented the artist with a picture of a native Texas species to copy.

During the transition to a museum from 1958 to 1966, Ima Hogg served as her own curator and, in her eighties, consulting with her old friend John Staub, planned and supervised the structural and superficial changes needed to convert what had been her home for nearly forty years to a public place. In 1961 she tried to describe some of the changes in a letter to Henry du Pont: "There is so much going on at Bayou Bend in the way of remodeling and shifting furniture around." She informed du Pont that Charles Montgomery, then director of Winterthur, had recently visited Bayou Bend and "pointed out many weaknesses in the collection, and I am having to reorganize some of the plans. . . . It seems I had concentrated mostly on Queen Anne and Chippendale furniture at the expense of Hepplewhite, Sheraton and the Federal styles. I really like what we are trying to do now much better, and yet I am a bit dismayed over some of the difficulties in procuring what I need."

In the archives at Bayou Bend is a typewritten progress report dated October 16, 1962, and addressed to S. I. Morris, the Houston architect who was then president of the Museum of Fine Arts. The report is signed "Ima Hogg, curator." In these pages she carefully described all the accomplished and proposed changes in the house, from the search for English delft tiles to frame the fireplace in the Massachusetts Room to the creation of a reference library for the

116

museum's docents. Many interior walls were rearranged; bathrooms and dressing rooms were removed or closed off so that visitors would walk through a series of spacious period rooms on the first floor downstairs and a more intimate group of bedrooms and sitting rooms on the second floor.

To make an entry for museum visitors from the terrace at the rear of the house, the breakfast room was converted to a hallway and its large window overlooking the terrace and reflection pool was made a glass door. The main rooms downstairs — the drawing room, the dining room, and the spacious hall between them — were left as they were. The Blue Room, once the Hogg brothers' sitting room, became the Massachusetts Room, with its vivid blue walls now setting off the patina of mahogany and the soft glow of burnished brass on the eighteenth-century Massachusetts-made furniture. The draperies in this room were to match the blue of the walls, and they were dyed three times before their color satisfied Ima Hogg. Adjoining the Massachusetts Room, where once had been the brothers' taproom, kitchen, and closets, interior walls were removed and one large room was created. This is now the Murphy Room, furnished with seventeenth-century pieces and dedicated to Katharine Prentis Murphy.

Upstairs, what had been Will's and Mike's bedrooms, bath, and dressing rooms became the Texas Room, the Federal Parlor, and the Newport Room. The idea of a Texas Room had actually been executed some years earlier, in the current Murphy Room. This early version of the Texas Room was opened, along with the Blue Room, on the annual Azalea Trail tour in March 1951. Until then, as a *Houston Press* story put it, the Texas Room had been "known only to the close friends of Miss Hogg." It was her first effort to create a museum setting. Here Ima could display her growing collection of Texian Campaigne ware, painted, glazed ceramic dishes made in Staffordshire, England, for the American market, depicting battle scenes from the Mexican War. This early Texas Room had a brick fireplace hung with iron pots and pans, chintz curtains at the windows, and a floor of large Shaker tiles.

The present Texas Room, now on the second floor, is patterned after a room used by General Sam Houston in the 1840s. The room is filled with memorabilia from the Mexican War, such as a selection of glass whiskey bottles and flasks bearing the likeness of General Zachary Taylor, the hero of the Mexican War who was elected president in 1848. There is a pitcher with Taylor's nickname, Old Rough and Ready, painted on it, and a portrait of the famous military hero hangs nearby. Here also hangs a portrait of Ima Hogg's paternal grandfather, Joseph Lewis Hogg, who fought in both the Mexican War and the Civil War. In this painting he wears his Confederate general's uniform.

Near the Texas Room a second-floor porch was glazed in to provide a midpoint rest stop and a magnificent view of the gardens for visitors on tour. The gardens themselves are a masterpiece in their own right. They were Ima Hogg's pride and joy. She was especially fond of the White Garden, a small informal area planted with nothing but white flowers — dogwoods, white irises, and billows of white azalea blossoms. It was here that she placed a small memorial stone in memory of Alvin Wheeler, her gardener for over thirty years. A later gardener, Kenneth Burkhardt, remembered how she kept an eye on the spring plantings and chores about the grounds from her upstairs window when she was busy with other matters indoors, occasionally signaling to the staff with a tiny whistle. When Hurricane Carla swept through Houston in 1961, uprooting trees and wreaking havoc, Ima Hogg's gardens were not spared. Henry du Pont wrote to her on September 12, 1961, "I do hope Bayou Bend is not damaged by the terrific hurricane!" The house itself was unharmed, and as for the damage to the gardens, Ima Hogg later relandscaped the spot where the most damage had been done and called it the Carla Garden.

In the conversion of the house to a museumlike setting, the other rooms upstairs were left virtually unchanged, except for the painstaking rearrangement of their contents to form a series of period rooms: the Queen Anne Suite, the Federal Parlor, and so on. Downstairs, the wide central hall, left intact and christened Philadelphia Hall, houses only Philadelphia-made pieces, some of the finest in the entire collection. Just off Philadelphia Hall is the former living room of the Hogg family, now converted to an elegant eighteenth-century drawing room. Here hangs Gilbert Stuart's portrait of George Washington; the likeness that every schoolchild knows gazes majestically from a crossetted frame on the wall above the mantel. Stuart is supposed to have made some fifteen copies of this portrait from the original, a painting of Washington commissioned for Samuel Vaughan of London in 1795. In 1921 one of these Stuart paintings was reported by the *New York Times* to have sold for $75,000 — then the highest price ever paid for an American painting. Since then American paintings have increased dramatically in value. In 1979, for example, Frederic Church's massive nineteenth-century seascape *Icebergs* sold for $2 million.

The Bayou Bend portrait of Washington is believed to have been the property of a William Patterson of Baltimore, who died in 1835. Patterson's descendants thought the portrait was a copy done by some anonymous artist, and the painting was finally sold, according to Bayou Bend records, for "a very nominal sum" to a dealer in 1959. The next year Ima Hogg bought it from Berry Hill Galleries in New York. In 1978, when the Boston Museum of Fine Arts and the National Gallery in Washington, D.C., were deep in negotiations over the custody of Stuart's portraits of George and Martha Washington, each claiming its city to be the only proper place for the portraits, the *Houston Post* carried an editorial observing with some satisfaction that Houston had its own Stuart portrait of Washington, "thanks to Miss Ima Hogg."

Downstairs in the corner of the west wing, adjacent to the dining room, is the Chillman Suite, often called the Empire Suite, since it is furnished in the style of the early 1800s (the empire referred to is Napoleon's, 1800–1812). Ima's friend Dorothy Dawes Chillman, whose husband, James Chillman, Jr., was the first director of the Museum of Fine Arts, Houston, worked closely with her on the furnishings. After Dorothy Chillman's death in 1968, the year the rooms were finished, Ima Hogg named the parlor and foyer for her. This room's massive pieces are far removed from the delicate style of the period that immediately preceded it chronologically, the Federal period. Typical of the Empire style is one of Ima Hogg's last acquisitions for the Bayou Bend Collection: a drop-leaf sofa table bought in 1972, made of dark mahogany and decorated with gilded carvings of caryatids, columns of acanthus leaves, and scrolls on the skirt and legs. There is a table almost identical to this one in the Red Room of the White House.

When the Empire Suite was completed, Ima Hogg directed the conversion of a cloakroom and powder room in the east wing, just off the gardens, to make still another display room. This new room became the Belter Parlor, named after the nineteenth-century cabinetmaker who created the furniture. It is an antebellum parlor replete with huge bouquets of red and gold roses on the Brussels carpet, heavy damask draperies, and an elaborately carved rococo settee and matching chairs.

All in all, the Bayou Bend Collection is an impressive achievement, and one that gives the beholder a sense of history that cannot be found in any book. Walking from the delicate, disciplined elegance of the Federal Parlor, with its pastel shades and its controlled rectangles and ovals; to the Empire Suite, with its emerald-green silks, heavy, curving shapes, and elaborately inlaid woodwork patterns; to the blood-red hues and rococo shapes of the Belter Parlor, one can almost feel

119

the Civil War coming on.

The Belter Parlor, the latest in chronology of the rooms at Bayou Bend, is actually the first room seen by tourist groups on the regular two-hour journey through the house. All visitors to Bayou Bend approach the house from the north side, crossing the gently swaying footbridge across the bayou and arriving at a glass-and-wrought-iron gazebo where an armed security guard sits in air-conditioned comfort. Brick pathways lead through hedges of miniature azaleas and beds of bright annuals to Winedale Cottage, a replica of an antebellum Texas building converted from the original gardener's cottage near the west wing of the house. Here the museum docents greet visitors, and here, in an anteroom neatly lined with metal lockers, guests leave handbags that could brush against a piece of seventeenth-century ceramic ware or an 1820s Tuckerware tea set. For female guests who may be wearing high heels that could damage a rare Kirman or Aubusson carpet, Bayou Bend provides knitted slippers, an unexpected bonus that one appreciates after the two-hour walk through the house.

Tours start at fifteen-minute intervals in groups of no more than four, and each group is led by a volunteer docent who gives an informal running commentary on the rooms and their contents. Although the comments are informal, the preparation for them is not. Bayou Bend's docents invest considerable time and effort in preparing to be knowledgeable guides through the museum's collections. There is no place here for the dabbler or the socialite. When David Warren, Bayou Bend's first curator, began to help select prospective docents, he was not taken in by social status or superficial knowledge. He once remarked that when he asked a prospective docent why she wanted to be one and she said, "Oh, I just think it would be a lovely thing to do," he was unimpressed. Docents at Bayou Bend must have a serious interest in Early American art and furnishings and must learn to analyze their appreciation of objects they admire. As David Warren put it, just saying, "Oh, I just love this lovely little thing because it is so lovely" is not enough.

Docent training at Bayou Bend involves thirteen weeks of classes with an examination at the end, plus an oral report and a research paper. Sample topics: "Texian Campaigne Ware," "Shaker Furniture," "The Queen Anne Card Table." The required readings for the course in 1979 were 5 books, 5 articles, and 3 longish excerpts from books; the additional suggested reading list contained 117 books and 63 articles. Classes meet once a week from ten to noon and from one to two-thirty. The trainees hear lectures, see slides, and do room studies, learning how to answer visitors' questions and give informal talks on the collection.

Bayou Bend's docents have a demanding dual role to play: they must be both gracious hostesses and security guards. At Bayou Bend nothing is roped off; nothing is labeled "Do Not Touch." One has the feeling of being a guest in an elegant home where a charming and knowledgeable hostess is showing off her treasures — except that, like the visitors, she herself is not allowed to touch anything. She carries a small flashlight, instead, to play over the intricately carved ball-and-claw foot of a tea table or the painted figures on a porcelain tea service. For emergencies, she also carries a tiny whistle.

When Bayou Bend first opened for regular tours on March 8, 1966, there were fifty-seven active docents; now there are more than four hundred. The first group was chosen by Ima Hogg; now the applications are reviewed by the curator and the chairman of the docents. Prospective docents are generally recommended by other docents, and are interviewed by the curator and the docent chairman. They must pass the rigid requirements of the prescribed course of study, and when they finish, they must make a commitment far beyond that of most volunteer workers. All Bayou Bend docents must agree to be responsible for leading at least one two-hour tour per week for thirty-six weeks a year, for five years — no matter what. Docents take twelve weeks at a time, with a month off in between, and there are no tours at all during August, when the museum is closed. They take the responsibility seriously: one docent, unexpectedly called to the hospital, said later, "There was my brother so ill, and all I could think of was how I was going to get a substitute for my tour the next afternoon." That so many docents are so dedicated to serving Bayou Bend is a tribute to Ima Hogg, who planned it all that way.

In the summer of 1961, five years before Bayou Bend officially opened to the public, Ima Hogg arranged for Jonathan Fairbanks to come to Bayou Bend to train the first class of docents. In July she wrote to Henry du Pont that Fairbanks, "a most personable young man," was "giving very thorough informal talks on the furnishings and background of each style or period to be found in the rooms here. Twenty-three girls attend regularly, take notes, and are very enthusiastic. These girls will be future docents when Bayou Bend is opened — time uncertain!"

While Ima Hogg was overseeing changes in the house and gardens at Bayou Bend, she also found time to accept the Amy Angell Collies Montague Medal for civic achievement from the Garden Club of America in 1959. That same year she was honored along with Henry du Pont and John D. Rockefeller, Jr., by the American Institute of

Decorators. In 1960 the Museum of Fine Arts, Houston, gave a special reception to honor Ima Hogg as the donor of Bayou Bend, presenting her with a special plaque commemorating her gift. At Bayou Bend itself, however, the gift was far from complete. In June 1961 Ima Hogg wrote to Henry du Pont, describing the ongoing changes in the transition from house to museum wing. "I am amused when you ask me," she wrote, " 'If you have any problems about furnishing, reorganization, etc., etc.,' I could not begin to enumerate!" She had her own furnishings to consider, too, for as she told a friend with some amusement when she was contemplating leaving Bayou Bend, "I don't have a *stick* of furniture!" To remedy that, she began to scout the furniture galleries in Houston before auctions. Taking Jane Zivley, her secretary, along, she would walk through the showrooms and whisper, "Get the number of that table . . . that chest . . ." Then she would have someone else bid, for if it became known that Ima Hogg approved of a piece, its value would go up.

For all her amusement at having to start from scratch in a new apartment, Ima Hogg had mixed feelings about moving to the high-rise complex at 3711 San Felipe. She was, after all, eighty-three years old, and Bayou Bend had been her home for nearly half her life. It was not an easy move, and after all her work, all the hundreds of painstaking decisions and arrangements, sometimes it seemed to those around her that she might not move out, after all. But as usual when things were difficult, she rallied, and one day in the fall of 1965 she walked out of the house for the last time, climbed into a waiting car, and went to her new apartment without once looking back. At the dedication of Bayou Bend she would say cheerfully, "Now I am free to pursue my other projects . . . and to watch the sunsets from a high-rise apartment." But she never stayed away from Bayou Bend for very long. Until she reached her nineties, she was fond of dropping in on Bayou Bend while tours were in progress, and many a docent was put on her mettle by having Ima Hogg suddenly join her tour group. In 1971, when a special tour group of docents from Winterthur Museum came to Bayou Bend, Miss Ima guided them through every room in the house and then accompanied them to Round Top, 120 miles away, to give them a personally guided tour of the antebellum restorations she was completing there. She was then eighty-nine.

On a chilly March morning in 1966, a dedication ceremony was held for the Bayou Bend Collection of the Museum of Fine Arts, Houston. Under a tent on the terrace were gathered several hundred guests and an assembly of distinguished speakers, including Governor John Connally, Mayor Louie Welch, Museum of Fine Arts director

Presents from the Past

James Johnson Sweeney, Charles Montgomery of Winterthur, and Harry Ransom, chancellor of the University of Texas. The first to speak was Ima Hogg herself. "Today," she said, "marks the culmination of a long cherished dream. . . . While I shall continue to love Bayou Bend and everything here, in one sense I have always considered I was holding Bayou Bend only in trust for this day." Some weeks earlier, Henry du Pont had written to her, "It is quite a shock leaving your home and having it become a museum. I went through all that some 14 years ago, but, I assure you, as time goes on, you will be more and more delighted with what you have done."

Once a project was finished, however, there was only so much energy Ima Hogg could devote to it, and without a new interest she often found herself at loose ends, idle and discontented. People who had known her for many years recalled how she used to languish without a project of some sort. There were times when she still suffered from depression, and there had been occasional periods when she did not leave her room at Bayou Bend for days or even weeks at a time. Then, as suddenly as they had come, the bad times would disappear; the energy would return; the telephones would begin to ring; the daybooks would fill up again with appointments and excursions. Perhaps it was the need to have a new interest that prompted Ima Hogg, shortly before leaving Bayou Bend, to tackle her most ambitious restoration project. At Winedale, Texas, about eighty miles west of Houston, was a ramshackle 113-year-old inn. In 1963 Ima Hogg bought the property, which included the eight-room inn, a barn, and some old slave quarters set on 130 acres in the gently rolling hills of Central Texas. The main building had once served as a stagecoach stop on the road between Brenham and La Grange. At first her idea was to restore the inn and move it to Houston, to the gardens at Bayou Bend. There the old structure, known as Sam Lewis's Stopping Place, could serve as a repository for the early Texas art and furniture she had begun to collect. Ima Hogg wanted visitors who came to see the Early American treasures of Bayou Bend to have the opportunity to become acquainted with Texas primitive furnishings from the nineteenth century as well. Moving and rebuilding the old inn, however, proved too difficult and too expensive, even for Ima Hogg. After consulting with architect Wayne Bell, who was to work closely with her on the entire project, she regretfully abandoned the idea of moving the buildings to Bayou Bend, and with her usual good humor and determination, she set about restoring the old structures on their original site.

Winedale, so named for its early German immigrant settlers' talents for making wine, is located just outside the tiny village of Round Top in northeastern Fayette County. The settlement is one of the oldest in Texas, dating from the 1830s, when land in the area was doled out to American settlers by the Mexican government. Some of the land was taken by German immigrants seeking a new home in the fertile farmlands of Central Texas. One of these immigrants was a man by the name of Soergel who came to Texas in the 1850s. He built a big farmhouse with a round tower that could be seen for miles around. Settlers eventually gave the name Round Top to the small village that grew around the Soergel place. Before the house with the round tower was built, the community had been called Josh's Creek Valley, after the stream that flowed into the larger Cummins Creek and then into the wide Colorado River. Gradually, as more people came, the place came to be called Townsend, after one of the first families that settled nearby. Later the name was changed yet another time, to Jones Post Office, to commemorate the addition of mail service to the community. Today, although Soergel's house with its round tower is no longer standing, the tiny town is still called Round Top.

By the 1850s there were 150 people living in Round Top, and the town had all the essentials for a thriving community: two blacksmith shops, two general stores, and two taverns. A stagecoach came through three times a week, and weary travelers could put up at a two-story cedar-timbered building known as Sam Lewis's Stopping Place. The inn was well known on the stagecoach runs from San Felipe to Bastrop and from Houston to Austin. Sam Lewis, the owner, made a comfortable living there from the time he bought the inn in 1847 until his death in 1867.

The sturdy old house that Lewis converted into a stagecoach inn had been built some years earlier. The land around the house had originally belonged to W. S. Townsend, who came to Texas from South Carolina in 1831 with his brother John. Another branch of the family had already settled near Round Top in 1826. In 1834 W. S. Townsend married a young lady named Mary Burnam, and he probably built the home for his new bride. It was a simple, sturdy building with two large rooms downstairs and a sleeping loft upstairs. In 1840 Townsend sold the property to Captain John York, an Indian fighter, who then sold it to Sam Lewis in 1847. Lewis, who had served as a representative from Austin County in the Ninth Congress of the Republic of Texas in 1844–45, decided to settle down in Round Top. He enlarged the house that Townsend had built, more than doubling its size, and in 1849 he opened it as a stagecoach inn for travelers on the road between Houston and Austin.

In the remodeling of the house Lewis built another identical cedar-timbered structure with two large rooms on the first floor and two above, and connected it to the original house with a dogtrot—a covered passageway that served as a convenient breezeway and porch in the hot Texas summers. Lewis also added a second-floor gallery across the front. The finished building, constructed throughout of massive cedar timbers—notched and pegged, not nailed—and with cedar siding on the exterior walls and a cedar shake roof, had four large rooms downstairs and four upstairs, divided two and two by the dogtrot. The kitchen was in a separate building in the rear. The inn was a roomy structure, but as time passed, travelers must have found it crowded. By 1850 Sam Lewis and his wife, Marshall Ann, had eight children—five boys and three girls, ranging in age from one month to seventeen years. Stagecoach passengers may have found a bed and a meal at Sam Lewis's Stopping Place, but it is unlikely that they found much peace and quiet.

Fifteen years after Lewis died, the family finally sold the inn to a German immigrant, a shoemaker named Joseph Wagner, in 1882. That was the year Ima Hogg was born. The Wagner family lived in the house until 1960, when Joseph Wagner's son, then ninety-one, sold the property to a Houstonian, Hazel Ledbetter, who sold it to Ima Hogg in 1963.

With architects Wayne Bell, John Young, and Drury Alexander, Ima Hogg set about restoring and refurbishing the old inn and its outbuildings, among them two cabins built of huge oak logs perhaps as early as the 1830s, when the Townsends had owned the property. At some later date the two cabins had been converted to a barnlike structure. The inn itself was discovered to have unsuspected treasures in the form of oil-painted floral designs around the ceilings of the upstairs rooms. The elaborate motifs were thought to have been painted sometime before the Civil War. Ima Hogg personally directed the removal of layers of old paint and the painstaking restoration of the designs. She also found a place in New England that could reproduce the heavy handmade nails used in parts of the inn's construction. She took a cottage nearby and spent her weekends there, climbing around the construction in progress and inspecting every detail. She was then eighty-one. Never one to waste time or energy, she used the two-and-a-half-hour automobile ride between Houston and Round Top to nap: curling up with a pillow on the back seat, she would sleep until the destination was nearly reached, and then, refreshed, she would be out and in command.

When at last the inn and the other restorations were finished to Miss

Ima's satisfaction, the Winedale property was dedicated and presented to the University of Texas as an endowed center for the study of Texas architecture, arts, and letters, as well as the ethnic history of the state. She searched the surrounding countryside for artifacts to exhibit at the dedication ceremonies in 1967. She put up notices in nearby stores asking for old paintings, textiles, quilts, tinware, and cabinet work to place in an exhibit of Texas decorative arts. She also arranged for a typical German-style oompah brass band to play. The principal speaker on the occasion of the dedication was Charles van Ravenswaay, director of the Winterthur Museum. Not long after Winedale Inn opened for use, Ima Hogg received the Texas Restoration Award and another state award for historical preservation. Said she, "I want Winedale to be a laboratory for the revival and restoration of a way of life."

Winedale today offers visitors a glimpse of what life was like for Texans before the Civil War, and the grounds have provided a picturesque setting for a unique spring music festival. One of the old converted barns was made into a hall for plays and concerts, complete with a stage and dressing rooms. In 1968 James Dick, a concert pianist and a close friend of Ima Hogg's, directed the first Fine Arts Festival at Round Top. The festivals have become increasingly popular over the years, and the facilities have been enlarged accordingly. In 1969, to celebrate the festival concerts, Ima Hogg gave a picnic on the grounds for four hundred guests. As usual, she thought of everything. There were sandwiches of smoked turkey and ham; there was homemade bread, cheese, potato salad, sauerkraut; there were cakes and apple cider and wine and cheese and nuts and cookies and, for the children, Eskimo pies. She was always a firm believer in nourishing the body as well as the spirit.

Not long after Winedale Inn was completed, Miss Ima began yet another project — the restoration of an 1860s house near Round Top. It had been built in 1861 by Dr. Gregor McGregor, a physician from North Carolina who came to Texas just before the Civil War began. Exempt from military service when the war came, McGregor stayed to serve his neighbors' medical needs and lived in the house until 1873. The house then passed through several hands until Ima Hogg bought it in 1969. The old structure had fallen into disrepair, and rather than attempt the restoration of it where it stood, she decided to move it to the complex of nineteenth-century buildings already at Winedale. The entire structure was dismantled and transported some fifteen miles to a site near the inn. The McGregor house, made of Eastern red cedar with mortise and tenon framing, was a sturdy, well-built house with three large rooms on the first floor and three bedrooms and a sitting room on the second. The kitchen, once again, was in a separate building. Restoration was painstakingly slow, but the results were rewarding. When three layers of paint on the interior woodwork were carefully removed, elaborate floral frescoes, similar to those in the Winedale Inn, were uncovered. The designs were done in bright-colored oils on a pale background, in a style common to some nineteenth-century German artwork, and they are thought to be the work of Rudolph Melchior, who came from Prussia to Round Top in 1853. He worked as an artist, paperhanger, and bookbinder, fought in the Confederate Army, and after the war moved to Galveston, where he died of yellow fever in 1868. Ima Hogg brought in a decorative painter trained in Germany to restore the frescoes. He also restored the painted wood-grain design on the doors and reproduced the marbleized effect painted on one of the fireplaces. In the course of the restoration one fireplace, built with handmade bricks, was discovered to have been boarded up. It was duly reopened and a new chimney built for it.

To furnish the house authentically, Ima Hogg relied on careful historical research. All the available estate records of men who died in Austin and Washington counties from 1855 to 1870 were studied to determine exactly what kinds of furnishings were popular in that part of Texas in the Civil War years. In an interview for the Houston Metropolitan Archives project in 1974, Miss Ima reminisced about her search for antebellum furnishings:

> I had one bed that was *given* to us. I wanted to buy it, and the lady said, "No, we have had many people want to buy this, but we would never allow it to be sold, because we want to keep it for a museum." I said, "This will *be* in a museum." "All right, you can have it!" Then I have another bed — it's a *glorious* bed — but made for the family by Steinhagen. He made it for his bride. He said it would never go out of the family. And a young woman down in — oh, right near here, in a little village — had it. . . . I went down to see it. It was a fabulous thing. I thought a long time, and finally I said, "I will *lease* this. I will lease it from you for ten years. At the end of the ten years, I'll give you more money for your heir — for any heirs you have." So it really will be ours, but not in name.

The bed that Ima Hogg leased belonged to the family of Christofer Friderich Carl Steinhagen, a German immigrant who became a wheel-

127

wright in Anderson, Texas, in the 1850s. As a hobby he made furniture for his family. The bed he made for his bride is a massive carved-oak four-poster with a matching child's trundle bed. It is now in one of the bedrooms of the restored McGregor House at Winedale.

The restoration projects at Winedale occupied Ima Hogg until she was well into her nineties, and she continued to take an active interest in Winedale until her death in 1975. She was never without enthusiasm and curiosity. She once told New York antiques dealer Harold Sack, when the two were admiring an ornately carved Victorian parlor set she had found for the Governor's Mansion in Austin, that the Victorian era's furnishings would be the next big fashion among collectors of American antiques. To Sack, who specialized in eighteenth-century pieces, she said, "You had better get with it!" She loved the new as well as the old: when the space program came to Houston in the 1960s she toured NASA and entertained the astronauts in her box at the symphony concerts; when her secretary complained about modern atonal music, saying, "You can't hum to it!" Ima Hogg dissolved in laughter. In the shocking sixties, she liked the Beatles' music and long hair on young men long before most people over thirty accepted either. Ima Hogg was always "with it." Former Museum of Fine Arts director James Johnson Sweeney once said of her, admiringly: "She stays on the bus!" Perhaps that was the reason she lived so long. The little girl who had ridden in a horse and buggy lived to see men fly to the moon; the young lady who came to Houston when it was a town of 75,000 people saw it grow to a metropolis of more than one million. For nearly three quarters of a century she had contributed to that city's cultural life in ways large and small.

Although Ima Hogg loved Houston, in later years she seemed to relish the rural life at Winedale and Round Top. At ninety, she signed up for a "farming weekend" symposium at Round Top, where there were to be classes and workshops on farm life in the Texas Hill Country. "I want to learn," she said, "how to mow hay." For her ninetieth birthday, friends in Round Top and in Houston established a sixty-acre arboretum near Winedale for the protection of rare and endangered Texas plants and wild flowers. It was just the right gift for Ima Hogg, who loved flowers almost as much as she loved music and art and people. From Houston, she once telephoned the curator of Winedale Inn early in the spring to ask if the wild flowers were in bloom yet. Busy and somewhat distracted, the surprised curator replied, "Oh, yes, Miss Ima, they are." But Ima Hogg was not to be dismissed so easily. *"How many?"* she demanded. A few weeks before her death in 1975, she attended the annual Fourth of July party at Round Top and lectured Houston's mayor Fred Hofheinz (who was not much more than one-third her age) on what he should propose at a mayors' conference he was planning to attend in Boston the next week. She was full of schemes for restoration projects all across the country. Old farmlands and orchards, as well as old buildings, she argued, should be brought back to life, and it was up to the cities to take the lead in historic preservation and restoration.

Ima Hogg's own passion for collecting and preserving the artifacts and structures of other eras left an impressive legacy. Winedale Inn, the McGregor house, the Varner-Hogg plantation, the Honeymoon Cottage, Bayou Bend: these are indeed presents from the past. "I can't remember when I was not interested in old things with a history," she once said. In 1966, the year that Bayou Bend was first opened for regular tours, Ima Hogg was given the Louise du Pont Crowninshield Award in recognition of "superlative achievement in the preservation, restoration and interpretation of sites, buildings, architecture, districts and objects of national historical or cultural significance." It is the highest award given by the National Trust for Historic Preservation and carries a citation, a trophy, and a stipend of $1,000. In October 1966 Ima Hogg wrote to Henry du Pont, "My dear Mr. du Pont (Harry): We spent some time in New York trying to find an object to buy with the Award check which should be a worthy emblem. We have about decided on a handsome and rare Bristol bowl painted by Fazackerly with Bianco Sopra Bianco border around the rim. I think it should be placed on a card table once owned by Governor Peter Faneuil of Massachusetts, which is now in my former Queen Anne sitting room."

That bowl is now at Bayou Bend, and the citation as well may be seen there, along with dozens of other awards and citations Ima Hogg acquired over the years for accomplishments ranging from establishing the Houston Child Guidance Clinic to serving as the first woman president of the Philosophical Society of Texas in that organization's 110-year history.

But she was always modest about her accomplishments, shyly accepting the honors that a grateful public showered on her. In a speech at the ceremony for the presentation of the Crowninshield Award she tried to share the limelight with others: "I grant you that in my limited way I have been given the good fortune to have initiated a few things, but I believe you will agree with me that a structure of enduring value is not builded by any one person alone." For this one person, however, the list of honors was long. In 1968 she was the first person ever to receive the Santa Rita Award from the University of Texas. This, the highest accolade bestowed by that institution, is named for the first oil well brought in on university property. It is given only to individuals who have assisted the advancement of the University of Texas System and the cause of higher education. In 1969, along with Oveta Culp Hobby and Lady Bird Johnson, Ima Hogg was one of only three women selected to become members of the Academy of Texas, an organization created to honor persons who "enrich, enlarge, or enlighten" knowledge in any field. That same year, 1969, she also received an award of merit from the American Association of State and Local History for her work in restoration. A few years earlier, in 1965, she had been named to an International Honors List for Distinguished Decorating by the National Society of Interior Designers, sharing the honor with Marjorie Merriweather Post of Washington, D.C., Baroness Philippe de Rothschild of Paris, and Princess Elvina Pallavicini of Rome. In 1972 the NSID presented her with its Thomas Jefferson Award for outstanding contributions toward the preservation of America's cultural heritage. When she was eighty-nine, Southwestern University gave her an honorary doctorate in fine arts.

As she entered her ninth decade, Ima Hogg seemed almost as young in spirit as she had at twenty or at seventy. Music continued to be — along with antiques — one of her passions. She loved it in all its forms, and hers was no dilettante's casual appreciation. Hearing the organ at St. John the Divine Episcopal Church, she might remark, "That was a lovely piece, but it would have sounded better with the diapason on full." When she visited a service at the Unity Church and the congregation joined hands during a hymn, Ima Hogg, caught up in the music, not only joined hands but began to sway back and forth, and soon the whole congregation was doing likewise. Her enthusiasm and sense of fun were infectious. Her sense of humor inspired her friend Howard Barnstone, a Houston architect, to give her a birthday surprise: while she was out, he filled the living room of her apartment from floor to ceiling with colored balloons. She was as delighted as a child. As she grew older she lost none of her fondness for shopping, lunching out with friends, and entertaining at home or at Bayou Bend. Up at six, she seldom went to bed before midnight, but in later years, on her doctor's orders, she consented to an afternoon nap.

Not long after her ninety-second birthday, Ima Hogg reminisced about her life and work in an oral history interview for the Houston Metropolitan Research Center. Her voice was strong and clear, her mind sharp, and her sense of humor as wry as ever, whether recalling a symphony conductor who "played some dreadful things" or describing the state of the plumbing at the Varner plantation. During that interview, in the midst of a serious discussion of the Houston Symphony's history, Ima Hogg, who had served her interviewer refreshments, spoke into the tape recorder with a twinkle of humor, "I like these doughnuts." She was obviously amused at the thought of this tape recording for posterity, but when friends later urged her to tape more of her reminiscences of building the Bayou Bend Collection and her experiences as a collector of antiques, she was adamant in her refusal. The Watergate scandal had been in the news for months. Said Ima Hogg: "That settles *that*! I'm not ever going to put *anything* on tape!" And she never did.

Although her strength began to wane in her last few years, she never lost her enthusiasm for collecting. On her trips to Europe she never failed to stop in New York to look over the latest acquisitions of her favorite dealers, even when she had to visit them via wheelchair. Her eye for craftsmanship and her search for perfection were as keen as they had been when she first began collecting. The summer before she died, she was still trying to add to a set of antique salt-glaze dinner plates she had found, and she kept her secretary busy telephoning all over the country in search of a dealer who might know the whereabouts of two more plates.

Although the stately *grande dame* of the 1970s had as much zest for life as the young girl of the 1900s, in later years she came to look on death with equanimity. Friends still remember an incident that took place when she was in her eighties. One afternoon when she was planning the dedication ceremony for the Winedale Inn, she announced that she was going to the country store in Round Top to see if the proprietress, an elderly woman named Mrs. Wagner, a relative of the Joseph Wagner who had once owned the inn, had any German music. Lucius Broadnax, her chauffeur, delivered her to her destination and then, at her suggestion, drove the rest of her party out to inspect some old slave quarters nearby. About half an hour later the group returned for Ima, who plied them with questions about beam construction and mortises and tenons, until finally one of the group remembered to ask if she had found her German music at Mrs. Wagner's. "Oh, no," came the answer. "Mrs. Wagner couldn't tell me. She was having a heart attack." She spoke as calmly as if Mrs. Wagner had been having a cup of tea. "I went into the store, and there she was, all blue in the face, and clutching at her chest. So I said, 'Mrs. Wagner, don't you have some oxygen here?' But she couldn't speak to me at all. So then I went next door and got her daughter and we called the doctor and the ambulance. She is getting better now, but I never did get to ask her about that German music. I think I shall send her an oxygen tank." Not long after that, a friend asked Ima Hogg what she was planning to do to celebrate the American bicentennial at Bayou Bend. She smiled, shook her head, and said, "Do you know how old I'll be by 1976? Ninety-four! No," she continued matter-of-factly, "I won't be here then." As usual, she was right. But in another sense she was wrong. As long as Bayou Bend, the Houston Symphony, the Hogg Foundation, Varner-Hogg Plantation State Park, Winedale Inn, and all her other projects exist, Ima Hogg will be here.

Sources

Note: In a work of this length, footnotes seemed an encumbrance. For anyone who is interested, there is an annotated copy of the manuscript in Doherty Library, University of St. Thomas, Houston, Texas.

Unpublished Primary Sources

Accessions Files. Bayou Bend, Houston, Texas.
Book of Family Letters, 1880–1904. Bayou Bend Archives.
Hogg, Ima. "Reminiscences of Life in the Texas Governor's Mansion." Hogg Collection, Eugene C. Barker Texas History Center, University of Texas at Austin.
Ima Hogg Interview, 1974. Tape recording, Houston Metropolitan Research Center, Oral History Collection.
James Stephen Hogg Papers. Eugene C. Barker Texas History Center, University of Texas at Austin.
Miscellaneous Papers. Bayou Bend Archives.
William C. Hogg Papers. Eugene C. Barker Texas History Center, University of Texas at Austin.

Interviews
The richest source of information for this work was the recollections of persons who knew and worked with Ima Hogg. The following is a list of individuals who provided valuable information in interviews, 1979–80.

Faith (Mrs. Charles) Bybee, collector, Ima Hogg's friend.
Ralph Carpenter, collector, Ima Hogg's friend.
Carl Cunningham, critic, the *Houston Post.*
Elva Kalb Dumas, Ima Hogg's friend.

Ima Hogg

Dean Failey, former curatorial assistant, Bayou Bend.

Jonathan Fairbanks, curator, American Decorative Arts Division, Museum of Fine Arts, Boston.

William B. Ferguson, attorney and chief financial adviser to the Hogg family.

Mary Fuller, Ima Hogg's friend.

Barry Greenlaw, former curator, Bayou Bend.

Ann Holmes, critic, the *Houston Chronicle.*

Tom M. Johnson, former general manager, Houston Symphony Orchestra.

Nettie (Mrs. Albert) Jones, Ima Hogg's friend.

Chester Kielman, former archivist, Eugene C. Barker Texas History Center, University of Texas at Austin.

Yvonne Coates Kleinsorge, Ima Hogg's nurse-companion.

Bernard Levy, antiques dealer, Bernard & S. Dean Levy, Inc.

Douglas McDugald, Ima Hogg's cousin.

Elizabeth (Mrs. Harvin) Moore, collector, Bayou Bend docent.

Betty (Mrs. Greg) Ring, collector, Bayou Bend docent.

Felide (Mrs. Charles) Robertson, Bayou Bend docent chairman, librarian, Ima Hogg's friend.

Harold Sack, antiques dealer, Israel Sack, Inc.

John F. Staub, architect of Bayou Bend.

Sandy (Mrs. Braxton) Thompson, Bayou Bend docent chairman, Ima Hogg's friend.

David Warren, first curator of Bayou Bend, associate director, Museum of Fine Arts, Houston.

Jane (Mrs. Walter) Zivley, Ima Hogg's secretary.

Secondary Sources

Amory, Cleveland. "Oil Folks at Home." *Holiday*, February 1957, pp. 52–56, 133–142.

Barnstone, Howard. *The Architecture of John F. Staub: Houston and the South.* Austin, Tex.: University of Texas Press, 1979.

Brightman, Anna. "The Winedale Stagecoach Inn near Round Top, Texas." *Antiques* 94 (July 1968), pp. 96–100.

Brown, R. B. "Furnishing a Home with Antiques." *House Beautiful,* December 1920, pp. 15–17.

Carroll, B. H. *Standard History of Houston, Texas.* Knoxville, Tenn.: H. W. Crew, 1912.

Cotner, Robert Crawford. *James Stephen Hogg: A Biography.* Austin, Tex.: University of Texas Press, 1959.

Sources

Downs, Joseph. *American Furniture: Queen Anne and Chippendale Periods.* New York: Macmillan, 1952.

Erdman, Donnelly, with Peter C. Papademetriou. *The Museum of Fine Arts, Houston: Fifty Years of Growth, 1922–1972.* Houston, Tex.: Rice University, 1972.

Frantz, Joe B. *Texas: A Bicentennial History.* New York: Norton, 1976.

Fuermann, George. *Houston: Land of the Big Rich.* Garden City, N.Y.: Doubleday, 1951.

Gambrell, Herbert. "James Stephen Hogg: Statesman or Demagogue?" *Southwest Review* 13 (April 1928), pp. 338–366.

Goldschmidt, Gretchen Rochs. "What Portraits Have You in Your Mental Picture Gallery?" *Alcalde*, November 1923, p. 363.

Halsey, R.T.H., and Charles Cornelius. *Handbook of the American Wing.* 5th ed. New York: The Museum, 1932.

Hogg Brothers. *Our Story of River Oaks.* Houston, Tex.: Hogg Brothers, 1926.

Hogg Foundation for Mental Health. *The Hogg Foundation for Mental Health: The First Three Decades, 1940–1970.* Austin, Tex.: Hogg Foundation for Mental Health, 1970.

Hogg, Thomas Elisha. *The Fate of Marvin.* Reprint of 1873 ed. Houston, Tex.: Premier Press, 1973.

Iscoe, Louise K. *Ima Hogg, First Lady of Texas.* Austin, Tex.: Hogg Foundation for Mental Health, 1976.

Kaplan, Barry, and Orson Cook. "Civic Elites and Urban Planning: Houston's River Oaks." *East Texas Historical Journal* 15, no. 2 (1977), pp. 29–37.

Katz, Harvey. *Shadow on the Alamo.* Garden City, N.Y.: Doubleday, 1972.

Katz, Herbert, and Marjorie Katz. *Museums U.S.A.: A History and Guide.* New York: Doubleday, 1965.

Kennedy, Mizell Ferguson. "A Study of James Stephen Hogg, Attorney-General and Governor." M.A. thesis, University of Texas, 1919.

Life, October 4, 1946.

Lockwood, Luke Vincent. *Colonial Furniture in America.* 3rd ed. 2 vols. New York: Scribner's, 1926.

Lomax, John. "Will Hogg, Texan." *Atlantic Monthly*, May 1940, pp. 662–672.

——. *Will Hogg, Texan.* Austin, Tex.: University of Texas Press, 1956.

McComb, David G. *Houston: A History*. Austin, Tex.: University of Texas Press, 1981.

McCraw, William. *Professional Politicians*. Washington, D.C.: Imperial Press, 1940.

New York Times, December 13, 1953; March 4, 1964.

People Today, July 4, 1950.

Pryor, William Lee. *"The Fate of Marvin*: An Epic Poem of the Civil War by a Texas Soldier." *Texas Quarterly*, summer 1977, pp. 7–21.

Roussel, Hubert. *The Houston Symphony Orchestra 1913–1971*. Austin, Tex.: University of Texas Press, 1972.

Sack, Albert. *Fine Points of Furniture: Early American*. New York: Crown, 1950.

St. Clair, Grady. "The Hogg-Clark Campaign." M.A. thesis, University of Texas, 1927.

Seal, Elizabeth Davis. "Is the Antique Fever Waning?" *Ladies' Home Journal*, March 1929, pp. 18, 85.

Spaeth, Eloise. *American Art Museums: An Introduction to Looking*. New York: Harper, 1975.

Sproul, Kathleen. *James Stephen Hogg: March 29, 1851–March 3, 1906*. Houston, Tex.: n.p., 1958.

Sweeney, John A. *Winterthur Illustrated*. New York: Winterthur Museum, 1963.

Taylor, Lonn. "The McGregor-Grimm House at Winedale, Texas." *Antiques* 108 (September 1975), pp. 515–521.

Taylor, Lonn, and David Warren. *Texas Furniture: The Cabinetmakers and Their Work, 1840–1880*. Austin, Tex.: University of Texas Press, 1975.

Terrell, C. V. "1892 Hogg-Clark Campaign." *Under Texas Skies*, March 1951, pp. 32–38.

Time, February 7, 1955.

Warren, David B. "The Empire Style at Bayou Bend: New Period Rooms in Houston." *Antiques*, January 1970, pp. 122–127.

——. *Bayou Bend: American Furniture, Paintings, and Silver from the Bayou Bend Collection*. New York: New York Graphics Society, 1975.

——. "Ima Hogg, Collector." *Antiques*, January 1982, pp. 227 ff.

Weber, Bruce J. "Will Hogg and the Business of Reform." Ph.D. dissertation, University of Houston, 1979.

Winchester, Alice, ed. *The Antiques Treasury of Furniture and Other Decorative Arts at Winterthur, Williamsburg, Sturbridge, Ford Museum, Cooperstown, Deerfield, and Shelburne*. New York: Dutton, 1959.

Sources

———. *Collectors and Collections.* New York: Straight Enterprises, 1961.

Wright, Roscoe E. "Tender Tempest — A Tardy Tribute to Will C. Hogg." *Houston Gargoyle*, September 21, 1930, pp. 6, 22–23.

Index

139

Index

Index